Operation

"REBIRTH AMERICA"
SECOND EDITION
BRAKE the WEB

By

America Publications
and
www.authorhouse.com

First published by AuthorHouse 09/13/07
Second Edition Published by AuthorHouse

ISBN: 978-1-4343-3397-1 (sc), Second Edition

Library of Congress Control Number: 2007906242

This book is printed on acid free paper.

For additional copies of this book;

• AuthorHouse, 1-888-280-7715

• www.authorhouse.com

• AuthorHouse
1663 Liberty Drive, Suite 200
Bloomington, Indiana 47403

DEDICATION

Operation "REBIRTH AMERICA is dedicated to all People as a reminder that the spirit of Liberty, Freedom and Justice for all People lives forever. It is a reminder of courage, vigilance and bravery to cause tyrants to tremble and flee. It is a collection of truth which confirms that…"the truth shall make you free."

Just For Today

*Just for today, I will live through the next 12 hours
and not tackle my whole life's problems all at once.*

*Just for today, I will improve my mind.
I will learn something useful. I will read something
that requires effort, thought, and concentration.*

*Just for today, I will be agreeable.
I will look my best, speak in a well-modulated voice,
and be courteous and considerate.*

*Just for today, I will not find fault with others.
I will not try to change or improve anyone but myself.*

*Just for today, I will have a program.
I may not be able to follow it exactly, but I will have it.
I will save myself from two enemies,
hurry and indecision.*

*Just for today, I will exercise my character in three ways.
I will do a good turn and keep it a secret.
If anyone finds out, it will not count.*

*Just for today, I will be unafraid.
Especially will I be unafraid to enjoy what is beautiful
and believe that as I give to the world,
the world will give to me!*

SCOOPIFIED
P.O.Box 277
Bellingham, WA 98227

Operation

"REBIRTH AMERICA"

* * * * * * * * * * *
CAUTION AND WARNING

Reading this book may cause a condition known as
COGNITIVE DISSONANCE or COGIZANT DISSIDENCE, "CD."

One of the most difficult things any of us can be confronted with is the fact that someone who we have placed our trust in has lied to us or betrayed our confidence.

When his happens, we often react in <u>total disbelief</u> or a <u>state of denial</u> by rejecting those thoughts we find too painful to bear.

Professionals call this reaction Cognitive Dissonance or Cognizant Dissidence, "CD."

As more and more people learn that some in their government, some religious leaders and others have been violating the peoples' trust and lying to them for years, CD grips many to the point that they are <u>incapable of a remedy</u>.

To counter the condition of CD, you MUST keep a <u>crisp, enthusiastic open mind</u> while you aggressively <u>seek the truth</u> and <u>then act</u> to correct the things needing correction.

* * * * * * * * * * *

President Franklin D. Roosevelt, (cousin of the Queen of England), said in the mid-1930s, paraphrased, "**NOTHING** happens in government **OR** politics **UNLESS** it is **PLANNED**." F.D.R. accidentally **EXPOSED** this **BIG "SECRET."**

Franklin Delano Roosevelt, "F.D.R."
32nd President of the United States
1933-1945

IDENTITY

Sun Tzu, 500 B.C., Chinese philosopher and general said, "If a man knows himself and knows his opponent, he need not fear a hundred battles. If a man knows himself and knows not his opponent, for every victory he will suffer a defeat. If a man knows neither himself nor his opponent, he is a fool and will suffer defeat in every battle."

And Jesus answered and said unto them,
"Take heed that no man deceive you. For many shall come in my name, saying, I am Christ; and shall deceive many. And ye shall hear of wars and rumors of wars: see that ye be not troubled: for all these things must come to pass, but the end is not yet."   Matthew 24: 4,5, and 6

General George Patton said,
"To be a successful soldier you must know history. Read it objectively – dates and even minute details are useless. What you must know is how man reacts. Weapons change but man who uses them changes not at all."

Operation "REBIRTH AMERICA"

PREFACE

He was twice elected, unanimously and unopposed, to the highest office in the land. His character, conduct and accomplishments throughout the seemingly short 67 years on earth, (45 of which were dedicated to serving his country since age 22), left him a reputation of great respect by friend and foe alike. He was saluted as:

First in war
First in peace
First in the hearts of his countrymen

George Washington established an example which many have attempted to emulate over the past 200 plus years.
During his two terms as the first President of these united States of America, he made notes on how to keep the enemies of America from destroying the Constitution and its Bill of Rights from without or from within.

He used these notes to compile **A WARNING TO AMERICA** known as his **"FAREWELL ADDRESS"**. The Farewell was never delivered as a speech. Rather, he had his scribes prepare enough copies of this 50 paragraph writing so they could be delivered, in advance, to every known worldwide newspaper editor. Each copy of The Farewell had a personal letter attached asking each editor to please publish its complete text on 19 September 1796.

He sent The Farewell by courier, by stage, by rider and ship. The editors complied, and the world received this superb and timeless warning document all on the same day. It was read from the pulpits, town halls and living rooms around the world. By the following week it was receiving rave reviews from throughout the land. This document quickly became **THE** guideline which kept America out of most of her troubles for nearly 100 years.

HOWEVER

It was this document, used by America's enemies, that taught them how to take over America from within. The three main areas determined by these enemies were:

1. Take control of the money
2. Take over the media
3. Take over the text book and law book publishing houses

**AMERICA'S ENEMIES HAVE DONE THIS –
LET'S TAKE HER BACK BEFORE IT IS TOO LATE!**

Pat Revere
America Publications Volunteer

*Dr. Paul addresses the U.S. House
of Representatives*

We Just Marched In
(So We Can Just March Out)

All the reasons given to justify a preemptive strike against Iraq were wrong. Congress and the American people were misled.

Support for the war came from various special interests that had agitated for an invasion of Iraq since 1998. The Iraq Liberation Act, passed by Congress and signed into law by President Clinton, stated that getting rid of Saddam Hussein was official U.S. policy. This policy was carried out in 2003.

Congress failed miserably in meeting its crucial obligations as the branch of government charged with deciding whether to declare war. It wrongly and unconstitutionally transferred this power to the president, and the president did not hesitate to use it.

Although it is clear there was no cause for war, we just marched in. Our leaders deceived themselves and the public with assurances that the war was righteous and would be over quickly. Their justifications were false, and they failed to grasp even basic facts about the chaotic political and religious history of the region.

Congress bears the greater blame for this fiasco. It reneged on its responsibility to declare or not declare war. It transferred this decision-making power to the executive branch, and gave open sanction to anything the president did. In fact the Founders diligently tried to prevent the executive from possessing this power, granting it to Congress alone in Article 1 Section 8 of the Constitution.

Today just about everyone acknowledges the war has gone badly, and 70% of the American people want it to end. Our national defense is weakened, the financial costs continue to drain us, our allies have deserted us, and our enemies are multiplying—not to mention the tragic toll of death and injury suffered by American forces.

Iraq is a mess, and we urgently need a new direction—but our leaders offer only hand wringing and platitudes. They have no clear-cut ideas to end the suffering and war. Even the most ardent war hawks cannot begin to define victory in Iraq.

As an Air Force officer serving from 1963-1968, I heard the same agonizing pleas from the American people. These pleas were met with the same excuses about why we could not change a deeply flawed policy and rethink the war in Vietnam. That bloody conflict, also undeclared and unconstitutional, seems to have taught us little despite the horrific costs.

Once again, though everyone now accepts that the original justifications for invading Iraq were not legitimate, we are given excuses for not leaving. We flaunt our power by building permanent military bases and an enormous billion-dollar embassy, yet claim we have no plans to stay in Iraq permanently. Assurances that our presence in Iraq has nothing to do with oil are not believed in the Middle East.

The argument for staying—to prevent civil war and bring stability to the region—logically falls on deaf ears.

If the justifications for war were wrong,

If the war is going badly,

If we can't afford the costs, both human and economic,

If civil war and chaos have resulted from our occupation,

If the reasons for staying are no more credible than the reasons for going,

THEN.....

Why the dilemma? The American people have spoken, and continue to speak out, against this war. So why not end it? How do we end it? Why not exactly the way we went in? We just marched in, and we can just march out.

More good things may come of it than anyone can imagine. Consider our relationship with Vietnam, now our friendly trading partner. Certainly we are doing better with her than when we tried to impose our will by force. It is time to march out of Iraq and march home.

F.R.E.E., Inc., P.O. Box 1776, Lake Jackson, Texas 77566, or call 979-265-3034.

FORWARD

Shortly after 9/11/01 our "ENEMY" was quoted as saying, (on National News), "the attack on the WTC and Pentagon was <u>NOT</u> against the American citizen, it was against the American <u>System</u>."

What is this "American <u>System</u>" he is talking about which has caused so much hatred around the world against America?

<u>Read on</u> and you will get a glimpse of what has been going on "behind the scenes" for more than 100 years – in America and worldwide – to set up this pre-planned hatred & wars, and how <u>YOU</u> can peacefully and Lawfully help bring the <u>REAL</u> America back!

1.   Some Americans have been saying, "I don't want to hear it. I can't do anything about it anyway!"

2.   Others are saying, "If we know who did it to us and how they did it, we can get America back <u>without</u> a <u>bloody</u> <u>revolution!</u>"

If you are among the <u>MAJORITY</u> of Americans who are in category <u>#2 above</u>, then read on. If not, then please pass this on to someone who is. Thank you.

<u>Note:</u> Over the past several years, Operation "REBIRTH AMERICA" has gone to:

1.	the USA President	8.	the FBI, CIA & BATF
2.	the USA supreme court	9.	International Truckers
3.	the USA congress	10.	International Bikers
4.	International activists	11.	The U.N, Fed, IRS & BAR
5.	All 50 USA states	12.	U.S. Secret Service
6.	County sheriffs	13.	International Media
7.	Local Police	14.	and others, including **<u>you!</u>**

<u>Just</u> <u>Do</u> <u>It</u>!!!!!

America Publications

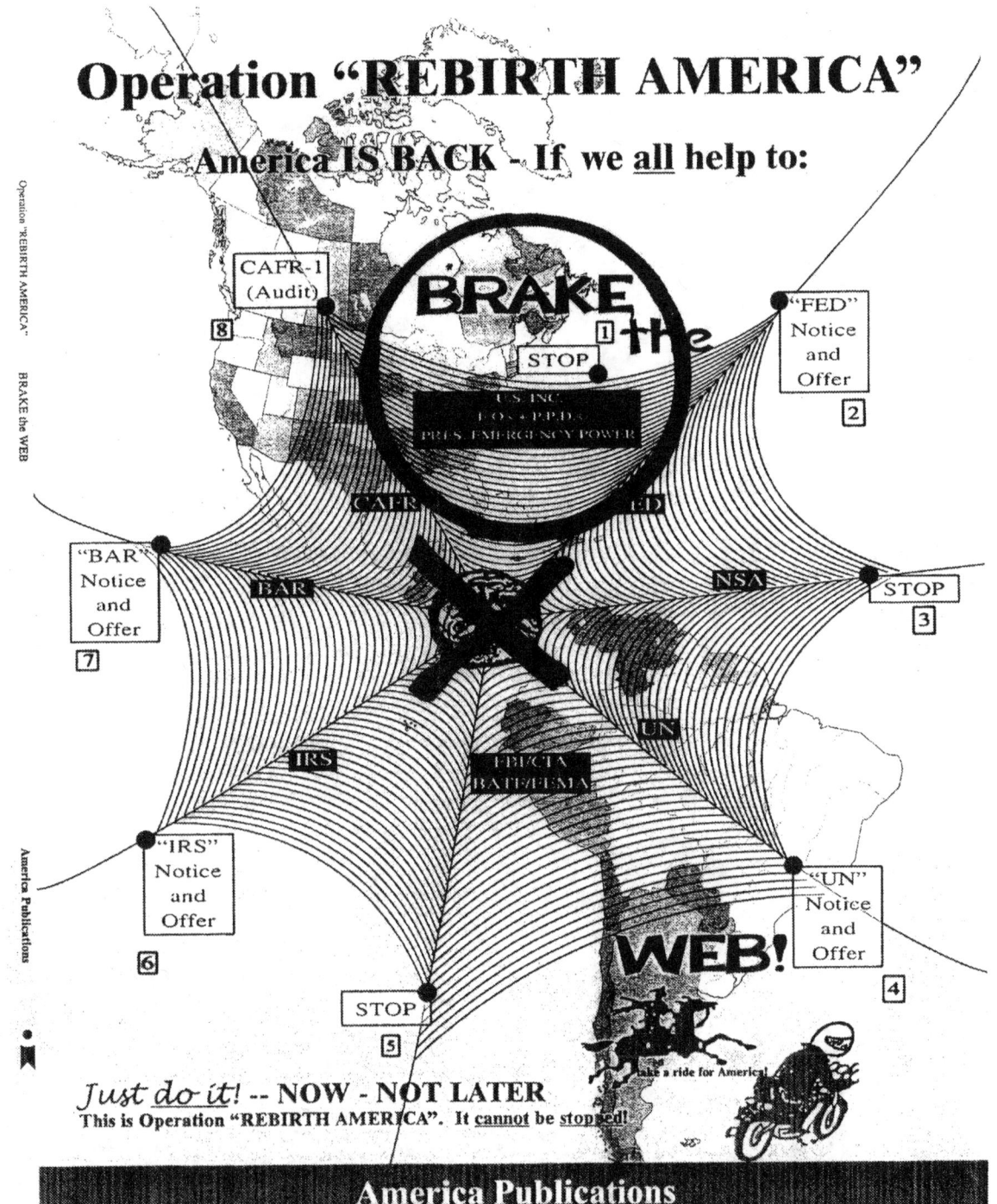

Operation "REBIRTH AMERICA"

America IS BACK - If we all help to:

Just do it! -- NOW - NOT LATER
This is Operation "REBIRTH AMERICA". It cannot be stopped!

National emergencies:

The United States of America was born in emergency. The Articles of Confederation were an emergency constitution. The Constitution for the United States of America was an emergency constitution. There have been great, pressing emergencies from time to time from the beginning, and likely will be for the entire duration of the nation.

The entire emergency power of the government was spelled out in the Constitution: Every emergency power is there, including unlimited war-making power, unlimited taxing power, and emergency power to suspend *habeas corpus*. The provisions are specific. There is, however, no contingency emergency power to enlarge emergency powers. There is no authority granted to go any farther than the emergency powers the Constitution specifies.

Every case, therefore, in which a President has said, "Well, we have to do it because this is an emergency," is a clear-cut case of usurpation and treason. Every such case is that of a limited government attempting to become an unlimited government.

We are always in the midst of a national emergency, and we shall no doubt always be so. The Constitution was written to make the government strong enough to commandeer the entire resources of the nation if needed to meet an emergency. Any President asking for more power is obviously more interested in power than in the welfare of the nation.

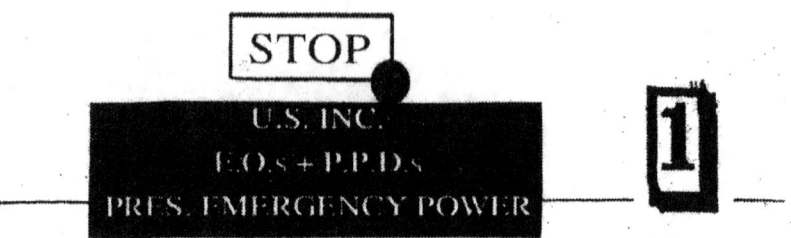

In September 1995, for the first time in American history, the inflow of tax revenues was less than our government had to pay on just the interest it owes. In other words, our Federal government can't even pay the interest on the loans they've promised to pay to mostly foreign entities. So, we decided to dig deeper into how this came about. What we uncovered is shocking, to say the very least.

It seems that the crafty powers that control this great land, behind the scenes, are about to choke us into submission. The <u>United States, Incorporated</u> declared bankruptcy, once again, in 1933. President Franklin D. Roosevelt, the author of American socialism declared this in <u>Executive Orders</u> 6073, 6102, 6111, and 6260. At the same time, all gold and silver was taken away from We the People. This was done pursuant to the Trading with the Enemy Act of October 6, 1917 when our entire nation was placed under an economic "<u>emergency</u>". Incidentally, this "emergency" has never been rescinded and we are still subject to the same "<u>emergency</u>" declaration today.

In order to bail out our insolvent federal government, the several incorporated franchise States of the Union pledged the faith and credit of We the People to the National Government. This is how we ended up with the Social Security Administration and the Council of State Governments, among many other socialistic entities. On January 22, 1937, these organizations published their Declaration of INTERdependence in The Book of States where they openly declared that all farmers (land owners) were no more than feudal tenants (page 155, 1937 edition). This was, and still is, the method used to literally steal private property from We the People in order to benefit others, without just compensation.

Today, a homeowner doesn't receive a lawful deed or title to his land. Instead, he receives a <u>Warranty Deed</u> whereby the State holds the actual title and deed as collateral for the National government's debt (the corporate body known as the United States located in Washington City). You don't own your land…the United States does. You only hold a piece of paper that warrants the original deed exists.

The same applies to motor vehicles. You are given a <u>Certificate of Title</u> when you buy a car, but the actual title itself is being held as collateral by the government. You are holding a piece of paper that certifies the title exists. In other words, even if you have no house mortgage or car loan, you still don't own them…<u>The United States holds title to your private property</u>.

The perverted Roman Civil Laws choked Rome to ruin, and America is following the same path. Under these <u>PPD's and Executive Orders</u>, the President may <u>seize property, organize and control industrial production, seize gold and silver, send military forces to foreign soil, institute martial law, seize and control all communication and transportation means, regulate and control all private business, and restrict all travel</u>. Basically, he can control the lives of every American in any manner he wishes.

Proclaimed "emergencies" have created over <u>470 Federal Law provisions</u> allowing the President extraordinary and UN-Constitutional powers through <u>Executive Orders</u> and <u>P</u>residential <u>P</u>roclamations and <u>D</u>irectives (<u>PPD</u>'s). This may explain why nearly every President has been a Bar attorney.

Your Signature Is The Most Important Thing You Own On The Face Of This Earth

The reason many of the first Christians died in the mouths of lions was that they refused to volunteer/sign a LICENSE/contract* for the worship of God! The power to give you PERMISSION, (sign/volunteer into a LICENSE/contract), is the power to CONTROL** and ultimately the power to TOTALLY PROHIBIT*** or ENSLAVE you!!

It's Time To Repair And Repent

*   IRS Code 501c3 for churches = voluntary govt. LICENSE/contract.
Driver LICENSE application = voluntary govt. LICENSE/contract.
Marriage LICENSE = voluntary govt. LICENSE/contract.
Social Security application = voluntary govt. LICENSE/contract.
Birth Certificate = voluntary govt. LICENSE/contract.
Voter registration application = voluntary govt. LICENSE/contract.
Passport application = voluntary govt. LICENSE/contract.

**   Gold fringed American flag = visible CONTROL or "quiet" military MARTIAL LAW by Executive Order #10834.

***   "Freedom From Religious Persecution Act," U.S. House HR-2431, (Senate version is S.772), deceptively sets up the Office of Religious Persecution Monitoring, "ORPM", = government and United Nations LICENSE/treaty/contract for FINAL CONTROL or PERSECUTION of ALL GOD-centered fundamental religion.

What Is The Uniform Commercial Code?

The Uniform Commercial code, "U.C.C.", is **NOT** positive law, (**NOT REAL** law)!

The U.C.C. is a confirmation that the Constitution of the United States of America, with it's <u>Bill of Rights</u>, has been circumvented and replaced by "<u>Civil Rights</u> and a National Corporate Democracy "Admiralty" court System.

<u>Civil Rights</u> are for National Corporate Democracy, U.S. <u>c</u>itizens **ONLY**, (small <u>c</u>). You **VOLUNTEER** to be a U.S. <u>c</u>itizen under <u>Civil Rights</u> – you were **NOT** born that way.

The Constitution and it's <u>Bill of Rights</u> are for Federal Constitutional Republic <u>C</u>itizens **ONLY**, (capital <u>C</u>), This is your **BIRTHRIGHT!!** You volunteer into something else when you **SIGN** a contract/license/**APPLICATION** in which state you are a U.S. citizen. Your **REAL** country of **ORIGIN** is the state you were born in, i.e., California, Tennessee, Pennsylvania, etc., you were born a <u>C</u>itizen of **ONE** of the **SEVERAL** states.

How Did We Get Two Different Governments?

President Franklin D. Roosevelt, (cousin of the Queen of England), said in the mid-1930's paraphrased, "**NOTHING** happens in government **OR** politics **UNLESS** it is **PLANNED**." F.D.R. accidentally **EXPOSED** this **BIG** "**SECRET**."

On March 9, 1933, these **PLANNERS** found a way – by **CREATING** an "**EMERGENCY**" and **TRICKING** the Congress to approve **TOTAL DICTATORIAL "EMERGENCY POWERS"** into the hand of President Franklin Roosevelt. ALL presidents since F.D.R. have had these **DICTATORIAL POWERS** to use – **ANYTIME** they choose to use them. These **DICTATORIAL POWERS** have allowed very powerful and greedy men and women to **QUIETLY**, and ever so **GRADUALLY**, change **YOU** and our government from a Federal Constitutional Republic, (which made America **GREAT**), into a National Corporate Democracy, which is bringing our **GREAT** country **DOWN** to a **SLAVE** state.

A U.S. <u>c</u>itizen belongs to (is a **SLAVE** to), the National Corporate Democracy.

A **FREE** American inhabitant <u>C</u>itizen belongs to **NO ONE** – the Federal Constitutional Republic works **FOR** the **FREE** American inhabitant <u>C</u>itizen. Democracy = Socialism = Communism = U.S. <u>c</u>itizen **SLAVE**.

If the license/contract/**APPLICATIONS** you have signed over the years did **NOT** fully disclose to you the above information, then these are **FRAUDULENT** "contracts" and you **CAN LAWFULLY** volunteer out of them and then **FILE SUIT** for damages!!

You can also help **PERSUADE** the current President to sign the "**PRESIDENTIAL PROCLAMATION**" which will **IMMEDIATELY END** his **EMERGENCY POWERS**, peacefully returning America to her **GREATNESS** in --- **LESS THAN 12 MONTHS ! ! ! !**

Presidential Document

Federal Register
Vol.____No.___

Presidential Proclamation No._____, this _____day of _____, _____.

The President   *Critical protection for the Constitution of the united States of America and its Bill of Rights by my cancellation and repeal, (by Proclamation), of the Emergency Powers Act of March 9, 1933, President Roosevelt's Proclamation #2038, #2039, & #2040, his Executive Orders #6073, #6102, #6111 #6260 along with HR 1491 of the same year*

———————

Presidential Proclamation

WHEREAS, as president of these united States of America, being of sound mind and body do proclaim the following as the truth, the whole truth, and nothing but the truth so help me God; and

WHEREAS, certain American protections are so vital that their incapacity or destruction would have a debilitating impact on the defense or economic well-being of these united States o f America; and

WHEREAS, I am extremely disgusted that no president before me had had the courage to cancel and undo the above MARTIAL LAW and ADMIRALTY WARTIME COURTS that President Franklin D. Roosevelt created when he signed the above documents and legislation into law; and

THEREFORE, I,   , hereby sign this Presidential Proclamation and IMMEDIATELY cancel the Emergency Powers Act and all related prior Presidential Proclamations and Executive Orders as stated above while proclaiming the national emergency has ended and all War Powers shall cease to be in effect as of this date; and

FURTHER, affiant saith not.

_____

President of the united States of America, this _____day of _____, _____ A.D.

WHY THE CHECK AND BALANCE SYSTEM HAS FAILED US!

The Public Administration Clearing House (P.A.C.H.) at 1313 E. 6th Street in Chicago was organized under the direction of a <u>socialist named Charles E. Merriam</u> who was funded by the Rockefeller family. The purpose of the P.A.C.H. has always been to bring all public officials <u>under one</u> <u>system of control</u>

The Rockefeller family provided 8 million dollars in the thirties to establish this clearing house so they could control the indoctrination of state-wide public officials, and <u>persuade</u> them as to the direction they ought to pursue, all the while, rendering themselves submissive to the <u>consolidated</u> <u>power</u> building up in Washington, D.C.

Merriam authored a book which was published in 1941 entitled: <u>On The Agenda Of Democracy</u>. In his book, Merriam defines *democracy*. It is what is also known as *communism!* He said revolution was "*the old way...the new way is education, persuasion, participation, and cooperation*". He taught how to achieve communism:

"Fortunately, our Constitution is broad enough in its terms, flexible enough in its spirit, and capable of <u>liberal enough interpretation</u> by <u>the judiciary</u> to <u>permit the adaptation of democracy</u> to <u>changing conditions</u> without serious difficulty."
"Legislative bodies are incompetent, it may be said, or corrupt, or dilatory, or unrepresentative of the general interest of the community."
"<u>The elective process is not favorable to the choice of the leaders of the community.</u>" ...Chas. E. Merriam

The Advisory Commission on Intergovernmental Relations (A.C.I.R.) was <u>grafted</u> onto the federal government in 1959. Its duty was to draft legislation to be handed to public officials all over the nation. <u>These were called "*slip bills*"</u>. Public officials were thus expected to get whatever was <u>handed</u> to them – passed into law! This made the public officials look like great thinkers to the folks back home! A.C.I.R. thus became the nation's *law-making factory*. In this manner <u>unified laws</u> were passed that took over. <u>Gradual consolidation of all power and control</u> was then achieved by public officials in Wash., D.C.

The governors also became members of P.A.C.H. and A.C.I.R. Their indoctrination and co-ordination for a "new world order" comes by their attendance at the annual "Governor's Conferences". Elections have been engineered that <u>those</u> who will co-operate (*with the desired power and other structural changes being sought to alter American Constitutional government*) <u>get heavily</u> <u>financed</u> and then moved into key positions of elected office.

During the services, all local control was moved to the federal level by <u>persuading</u> local and state officials to accept federal revenue <u>sharing</u> funds and to adopt "<u>general</u> <u>plans</u>" for cities and communities. <u>These must comply with the federal mandates set down for socialism and centralized control.</u> Having achieved the objective of acquiring all control over every aspect of American government, including people, land, armed forces, etc., the federal government has devised ways by which it now <u>transfers</u> (what it has formerly consolidated unto itself) <u>to the United Nations through</u> *purported* "treaties" to empower the United Nations <u>to have complete control over the "New World Order"</u> government. Included in the plan is <u>gradual</u> abolishment of states, cities, counties and land ownership. The nation's <u>governors</u> quietly <u>co-operate in the</u> <u>planned arrangement</u> for the <u>dissolution</u> of the very <u>states</u> they were elected to <u>Preserve, protect, and defend.</u> State officials were *supposed* to keep the federal system in check! <u>They have actually joined in the subterfuge!</u>

UNLAWFUL HOME FORECLOSURES

Some readers may recall reading how Jerome Daly achieved widespread attention over 20 years ago when a trial was held in the court of Credit River Township in Minnesota, that prevented a bank from seizing and selling his home because he was delinquent on some mortgage payments. Daly's defense was that the bank had not lent him any actual money, but had simply created credit on its books by the technique of fractional reserve banking; and that, therefore, since nothing of value had been advanced by the bank, it was not entitled to seize an asset consisting of real estate as a forfeiture. Banks do not lend money deposited by their customers. The president of First National Bank of Montgomery, MN, which is a member of the Federal Reserve Bank of Minneapolis, admitted that the Bank created the money and credit upon its own books by which it acquired or gave as consideration for the Note; that this was standard banking practice; that the credit first came into existence when they created it; and that he knew of no United States Statutes which gave them the right to do this. A jury of farmers sided with Daly, and he retained his property.

The Minnesota Trial Court declared the Federal Reserve Act, the National Banking Act and the mortgage extended to Daly by the Bank, along with the foreclosure and the sheriff's sale to be unconstitutional and Void. The bank did not appeal.

For decades, the courts, the Fed and the politicians have kept this burning issue under wraps. But now that foreclosures have become quite common, especially among farmers, there is a concerted movement to prevent the seizure of property. An increasing number of citizens whose property has been sold at sheriff's auctions are still occupying them, pending the outcome of lawsuits which have been filed against the banking institutions for fraud because of violations of the *Truth-in-Lending Act* and other very significant reasons.

We learn, for example, that Barbara Jasso of Michigan was still occupying her property sold by the sheriff 14 months previously. Frank Verhoffs family in Alabama was still operating its farm which was auctioned in the same manner more than a year earlier. Both have filed suits and no eviction seems possible while these are pending. They are demanding jury trials and must, under the law, be given the benefit of these. Jerry Wright of Colorado has filed a $100-million suit against the bank and the Farmers Home Administration, charging them with fraud. Wright's property was sold at auction. But he is still operating it, pending the outcome of his litigation. Many other suits have been and are being filed. Not one has come to trial and no one who has taken such action has been evicted. The banks fear such trials, which is not difficult to understand.

These are the principle charges being leveled against the banks: Since no actual money has been lent, they are in violation of Art. 1, Sec. 10 of the U.S. Constitution. Federal Reserve Notes are NOT dollars, and Congress had no jurisdiction to authorize the Federal Reserve to create such or issue bills of credit. Since the banks never lent any real money at all, but merely advanced credit created out of nothing on their books, they have no right to seize any real estate. Curiously enough, the courts, including the highest, have declared on numerous occasions that "credit" money is not lawful currency. And thereby hangs a crucial issue which must eventually be resolved. If enough people reject banks' bogus claim on
. their real property the monetary system in the United States will have to be returned to pre-Federal Reserve status to meet Constitutional requirements.

The banks have now loans so created totaling over $2 trillion, on which they collect more than $200 billion a year in interest. Thus we find that over 90% of our 'money" in existence is only checkbook or debt money. Banks are insatiable parasites that feed on all of us by incessantly generating more and more inflation that keeps reducing the purchasing power of our currency. They thrive by being allowed to steal from the entire nation.

For more information visit: www.mortgagefree4u.com/daly_decree.htm
www.mortgagefree4u.com/credit_river _decision.htm
www.lectlaw.comlfiles/ban11.htm

For additional information do a web search for "Jerome Daly Credit River."

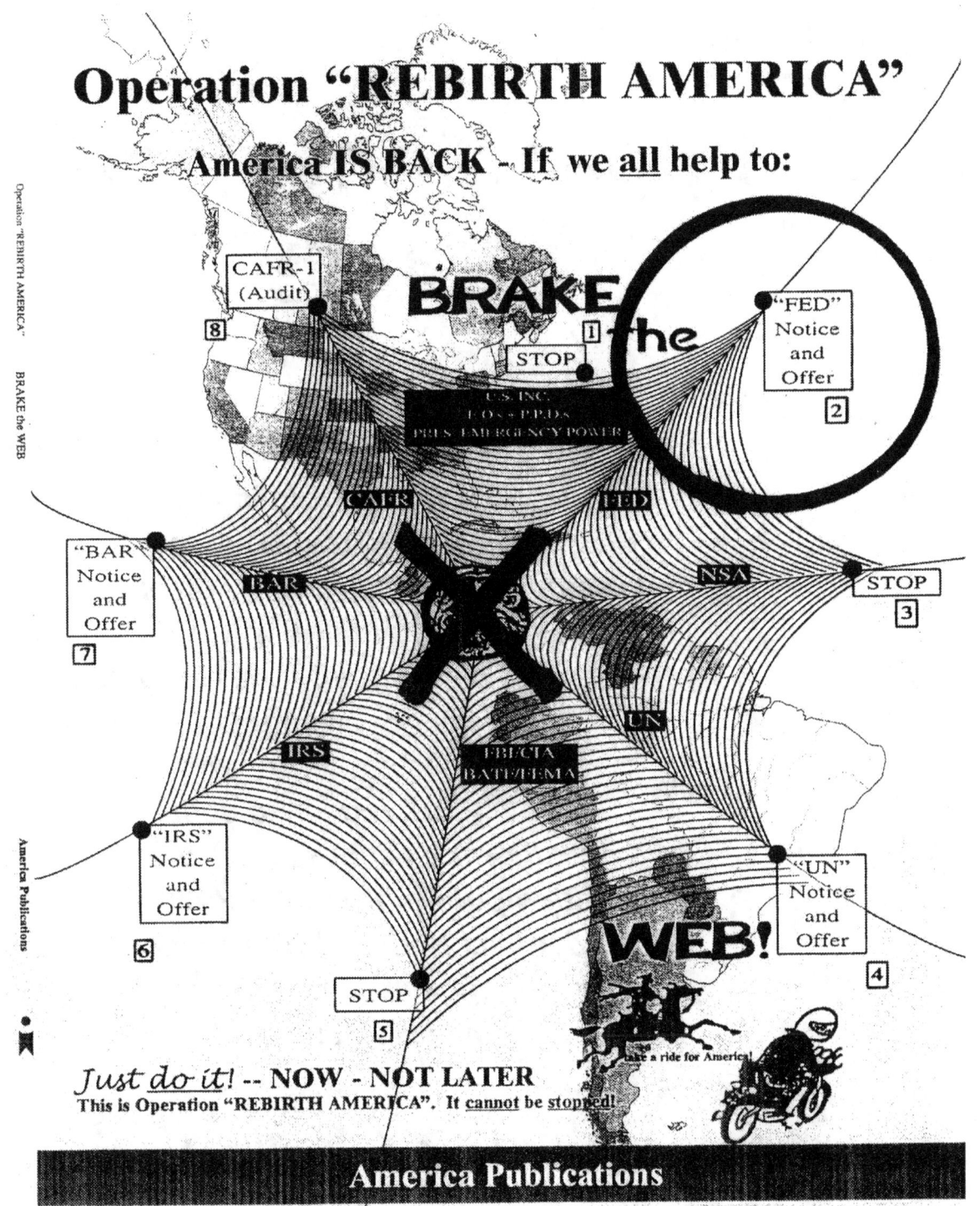

Operation "REBIRTH AMERICA"

America IS BACK - If we all help to:

BRAKE the WEB!

CAFR-1 (Audit) — 8

STOP — 1

"FED" Notice and Offer — 2

"BAR" Notice and Offer — 7

STOP — 3

"IRS" Notice and Offer — 6

"UN" Notice and Offer — 4

STOP — 5

U.S. INC.
E.O.s - P.P.D.s
PRES. EMERGENCY POWER

Just do it! -- **NOW - NOT LATER**
This is Operation "REBIRTH AMERICA". It cannot be stopped!

Take a ride for America!

Paper Money and Tyranny

*No one would welcome a
counterfeiter to town, yet this
same authority is blindly given
to our central bank without
any serious oversight by the Congress.
When the government can
replicate the monetary unit at
will without regard to cost,
whether it's paper currency or
a computer entry, it's morally
identical to the counterfeiter
who illegally prints currency.
Both ways, it's fraud.*

Foundation for Rational Economics and Education
P.O. Box 1776 • Lake Jackson, TX 77566
(979) 265-3034

Fax this to the White House — 1-202-456-2461

Fax this to the Senate — 1-202-224-2262

Fax this to the House of Representatives — 1-202-225-0697

Tell them to tell the Federal Reserve ("The FED") –

"FED, you and your agenda are finished in America. Get out and stay out!"

(Or, fax this directly to the FED yourself.)

-- Federal Reserve (private!) Banks --

Washington, DC	Fax 1-202-452-3819	Chicago	Fax 1-312-322-5515
Boston	Fax 1-617-973-5918	St. Louis	Fax 1-314-444-8503
New York	Fax 1-212-720-1216	Minneapolis	Fax 1-612-204-5273
Philadelphia	Fax 1-215-574-4114	Kansas City	Fax 1-816-881-2569
Cleveland	Fax 1-216-579-2477	Dallas	Fax 1-214-922-6500
Richmond	Fax 1-804-697-8123	San Francisco	Fax 1-415-393-1920
Atlanta	Fax 1-404-521-8050		

(Also FED employees and others)

NOTICE AND OFFER

We Americans hereby <u>notify</u> you that we <u>offer</u> that you, the Federal Reserve Banks, aka "FED" (lesser-known as the "<u>Glass Act of 1913</u>") complete amnesty if you permanently close down and vacate your offices for the following reasons:

- That you, FED, were secretly, fraudulently contrived on Jekyll Island in 1910;
- That you, FED, have committed treason against America;
- That you, FED have illegally and unlawfully since 1913 converted American Constitutional money into worthless fiat debt paper; "Federal Reserve Notes".
- That you, FED, have illegally and unlawfully conspired with the international banking cartel while using the private bank of the United Nations, the International Monetary Fund (IMF), to do your dirty work in stealing wealth from Americans and other people throughout the world;
- That you, FED, have illegally and unlawfully, by using "color of law" (which means no law at all!) used political action committees (PACs) to bribe officials into a "code of silence" to keep their mouths shut about your FED fraud.
- That you, FED, together with your directors, the evil private international banking cartel (also using the private bank of the U.N., called IMF) plan to economically enslave the people of America and the rest of the world by
- keeping them barefoot, broke, anxious, exhausted and downtrodden. This, by using the top secret Central Intelligence Agency (CIA) program called Methods Of Control, (MOC) -- forcing people worldwide into induced poverty and economic stress.
- NOW THEREFORE, WE <u>NOTIFY</u> YOU THAT WE <u>OFFER</u> YOU COMPLETE AMNESTY IF YOU CLOSE DOWN OPERATIONS IN
- THE UNITED STATES IMMEDIATELY.

"I had never thought the Federal Bank System would prove such a failure. The country is in a state of irretrievable bankruptcy."
—Senator Carter Glass, June 7, 1938

"Whoever controls the volume of money in any country is absolute master of all industry and commerce."
— President James A. Garfield

The Governor of each State grants "AMNESTY".

The Bank of England

The American Revolutionary War was fought against King George III of England not against the Bank of England. <u>The United States</u> won political independence from King George III but it <u>did not win financial independence from the Bank of England</u> of which King George III was a major stockholder. King George lost the American colonies but retained the banking control and continued to receive his interest and profits from his former American colony just as before. But no one seemed to mind very much because most people did not know about it.

Alexander Hamilton reestablished the Bank of England's presence in the United States immediately after the American Revolution with <u>the 1st Bank of the United States</u> that Thomas Jefferson strongly opposed. After Jefferson became President he refused to renew the charter of this foreign Central Bank so it went out of existence. In revenge England declared war on the U.S., the war of 1812, which was a banking war not a naval dispute. The Bank of England punished the United States for refusing to renew the charter of the 1st Bank of the United States.

The 1st Bank of the United States disappeared and then later Nicholas Biddle, an agent of the banking house of Rothschild, chartered <u>the 2nd Bank of the United States</u> that did quite well until President Andrew Jackson came along and said to the bankers, "You are a nest of vipers and by God I will rout you out." He removed all of the government deposits from the 2nd Bank of the United States in 1836, which caused it to collapse. In revenge the Bank of England suspended all American paper, which caused the first great depression in the United States called the Panic of 1837. Afterwards the Rothschild's agents and other agents of the merchant bankers in the City of London bought up American securities at about one cent on the dollar and established many of the great American fortunes like J.P. Morgan and associates.

The idea had always been advertised and promoted that the Rothschilds and the Bank of England had no activities in the United States, and it appeared this way because they worked through August Belmont who was their named representative, and they also worked through J.P. Morgan Company and Kuhn Loeb Company, which were their secret representatives. By 1896 these two Rothschild firms J.P. Morgan and Kuhn Loeb Co. owned 96% of all the railroad mileage in the U.S., as stated in U.S. Congressional Reports.

<u>The 3rd Bank of the United States</u> was called by a different name, <u>the Federal Reserve System</u>. The Federal Reserve Act was passed in 1913 which divided the United States into 12 Federal reserve districts in each of which is a Federal Reserve Bank. The stock of each Federal Reserve bank was sold to the commercial banks in each of the 12 districts. There have been mergers and transfers but because the Federal Reserve System was set up as a monopoly the stock could not be publicly bought, sold, nor traded. If one of these commercial banks that held Federal Reserve Bank stock went out of business that stock had to be returned to the Federal Reserve. However, *the stock of the commercial banks is privately owned*. About one hundred of the world's dynastic ruling families control the stock, and profit from the Bank of England-Federal Reserve international banking cartel.

The money center bank of the Federal Reserve System has always been the Federal Reserve Bank of New York. The other banks have merely rubber stamped whatever monetary proposals were advanced by the President of the Federal Reserve Bank of New York. The official Organization Certificate of the Federal Reserve Bank of New York dated May 19, 1914 shows six commercial banks actually bought control of the Federal Reserve System. Of the 203,053 shares issued, the Rockefeller and Kuhn Loeb controlled bank, National City Bank (later called Citibank) bought 30,000 shares. J.P. Morgan's First National Bank bought 15,000 shares. When these two banks merged in 1955 as Citibank, the nation's largest bank, they owned one-fourth of the total shares of the Federal Reserve Bank of New York. Chase National Bank (later called Chase Manhattan) bought 6,000 shares. National Bank of Commerce bought 21,000 shares. Hanover Bank (later called Manufacturers Hanover) bought 6,000 shares. Chemical Bank bought 6,000 shares. The controlling stock of the Federal Reserve Bank of New York was bought by these six commercial banks who, in turn, were governed by merchant banks in the City of London who, in turn, were licensed by the Bank of England.

Americans were deluged with much media publicity after WW II that Great Britain was giving up her empire. in fact, the British Raj, <u>the Bank of England</u>, and sundry global financiers ditched their more unprofitable colonial outposts because <u>they had recovered near total control over their most profitable overseas colony—the United States of America.</u>

The Federal Reserve

Today, America has a debt-based banking system called the Federal Reserve where money is created by government and private debt. <u>The Federal Reserve is not "Federal."</u> The name is a deception created before the Federal Reserve Act was passed to make Americans believe that America's Central Bank operates in the public interest. <u>The Federal Reserve is a private bank</u> owned by private stockholders and run for their private profit. The Federal Reserve also has doubtful reserves. <u>The Federal Reserve</u> is more powerful than the Government. <u>It is more powerful than</u> the <u>President</u>, the <u>Congress</u>, and the <u>Courts</u> because the Federal Reserve determines the average person's house payment, car payment, and whether they will have a job or not. <u>The Federal Reserve has a monopoly over U.S. currency</u> and it creates money out of nothing. Also, <u>the Federal Reserve is the largest single creditor of America's national debt.</u>

It is currently <u>impossible</u> for America to get out of debt under the present Federal Reserve System of bond-based government finance. Government bonds are promises to pay, i.e., IOUs. People buy bonds to get a secure rate of interest. At the end of the term of the bond the government repays the bond plus interest and the bond is destroyed. There are trillions of dollars worth of these bonds, i.e., loans, at present. <u>The solution</u> to America's indebtedness *does not* lie in discussing the "size" of the national debt, "deficits," or government spending—it lies in <u>reforming America's banking system</u>. Anything else is a deception by Federal Reserve cheerleaders in America's ethically and morally mortgaged media. The Fed perpetuates the national debt by making the American people borrow the money from the Fed at interest to pay the debts that have already been accumulated. Under the present system America's national debt cannot be extinguished without extinguishing America's money supply. Paying off the national debt without reforming the nation's banking system is an impossibility.

How does the Federal Reserve create money out of nothing? The Fed increases the amount of money in the economy when the Federal Reserve Open Market Committee approves the purchase of bonds and other securities on the open market. These bonds are purchased by the Fed from whoever is offering them for sale on the open market. The Fed pays for the bonds with electronic credits to the seller's bank, which in turn credits the seller's bank account. These credits are based on *nothing* except computer blips.

The commercial banks then use these deposits as reserves, which they issue loans against. Currently, they can immediately lend out more than ten times the amount of their reserves to new borrowers, all at interest. In this way a Fed purchase of, for instance, one million dollars worth of bonds gets turned into more than ten million dollars in bank accounts. The Fed creates 10% of this totally new money and the banks create the other 90%—from nothing but electronic and paper ledger entries. <u>The Fed</u> delegates to the commercial bankers and the right to create 90% of America's money supply <u>based only on bookkeeping</u> fractional reserves, which the bankers then lend out at interest. Commercial bank reserves are fictitious funds evidenced by figures on banks' books, which two authorities create: the Government when it issues bonds or bills of credit, and the Federal Reserve banks when they write a check against no tangible funds.

Conversely, to reduce the amount of money in the economy the process is just reversed. The Fed sells bonds to the public and the money flows out of the purchaser's local bank and out of the economy. Thus, bank loans must be reduced by ten times the amount of the sale. A Fed sale of one million in bonds results in ten million dollars less money in the economy.

The Federal Reserve creates the "business cycle" by lowering interest rates which produces an expansion of credit, higher prices, and rising stock market. After people are adjusted to these inflationary conditions, the Fed can check prosperity by arbitrarily raising interest rates. <u>The Fed causes</u> the pendulum of "<u>Boom</u>" <u>and</u> "<u>Bust</u>" to swing gently or violently by making small or large changes to the discount rate. It <u>possesses inside information</u> on financial conditions and advance knowledge of coming changes in the economy. <u>The pawns</u> in the "business cycle" game <u>are the working and producing people of the nation.</u> The beneficiaries are the wealthy elitist stock market gamblers who win or lose billions of dollars annually, but <u>the Fed manipulators of the game</u> lost nothing.

<u>The Federal Reserve manipulates</u> the amount of money in circulation <u>for the profit of a</u> <u>private privileged class of financiers,</u> and it has a high degree of independence from *effective* political control. The <u>Federal Reserve is part of an independent Super-State</u> controlled by international bankers, transnational corporations, and global business elitists <u>all acting together</u> <u>to enslave the world for their own pleasure.</u>

England (since 1815)	U.S. (since 1913)
"The City"* (of London) is 1 sq. mi. and it is controlled by the CROWN. The CROWN is NOT the Royal Family. It is 12 to 14 men with a Lord Mayor who is OVER the Queen or the King and Parliament.	Washington (Dist. of Columbia) is 10 mi. sq. and it is controlled by the FEDERAL RESERVE BOARD "FRB!*. The FRB is men who take orders from the CROWN and are OVER the President, the Congress and U.S. citizens.

*"The City", "FRB" and "IMF" are ENDING Liberty and Freedom.

The Death of Their "Money Tree" and how it CAN and MUST work

Have you ever wondered why the nicest, tallest and most expensive buildings in any city are owned by banks?

For 305 years the "private" bankers of the world have done this to the people of this planet with relative ease. HOW have they gotten away with this for ALL these years? Because YOU and I (and our ancestors) have been SOUND ASLEEP for 12 GENERATIONS!

It IS TIME to CANCEL "Usury/Interest Loan Banking" just as King William started it - - DEMAND "Simple Fee Loan Banking" TOMORROW MORNING, and DON'T say it can never happen, Usury/Interest banking is AGAINST Biblical (God's Law) and, up until the year 1694 when King Willie pulled this off, Usury/Interest banking was AGAINST the law in most countries in the world and was PUNISHABLE BY DEATH!

As a result of Usury/Interest loans being permitted all these 305 years, the PRE-planned "OCTOPUS of poverty" has reached deeply inside every continent on earth.

Today in the united States of America, a 30 year, $60,000 Usury/Interest loan requires you to pay back about $255,931.00 over the next 30 years of the life of that loan. If we DEMAND ALL banks RETURN to "Simple Fee" bank loans, (TOMORROW MORNING), no-one would loose his/her job and the bankers would not "receive "$195,931.00 in Usury/Interest. (A SIMPLE FEE for a $60,000, 30 year loan could be $6,000, or a $100 fee for each $1,000 of the loan amount). WHAT?, you ask, will become of existing loans? The answer is very, very simple. Banks will shift IMMEDIATELY to a "SIMPLE FEE" procedure for ALL existing and future loans. All existing loans will become "Paid-In-Full" if the "principal" and the "new" SIMPLE FEE have been paid, (however, to make the transition as smooth as possible, existing loans which have paid more than the "principal" and the "new" SIMPLE FEE, you would NOT get any money back, (the loan would just become – "Paid-In-Full"). This will allow the SIMPLE FEE loan transition to proceed without anarchy or war and become a Blessing for children and ALL generations to come.

Impossible you may say? Well, if It's God's Law, how can we say, "it's impossible"? Remember, it was King "Willie" who broke God's Law. It is my understanding from His words in the Bible God forgives and Blesses those who repent to Him in prayer as they return to His Law.

```
ANCIENT MYSTERY RELIGIONS ──── ...of Babylon, Egypt,
                                India, Persia, Greece,
                                etc. All were forms of
                                PANTHEISM

KABBALISM

              GNOSTICISM ──── Witchcraft, Sorcery,
                              Divination, Spiritism,
MARXISM                       most Occult
                              Practices, Eastern
American and  KNIGHTS TEMPLARS Religions (Hinduism,
European Secret               Buddhism, Shintoism,
Political Societies           etc.)
              ROSICRUCIANS
PRIVATE
International
Banking Elite  FREEMASONRY / ILLUMINATI ──── 1782

World Council of                New Spiritual
Churches     Theosophical  Many cults   Technology (Flotation
             Society       of the       tanks, self-hypnosis
                           1800's       tapes, subliminal
                                         persuasion, etc.) ←── NSA

              NEW AGE MOVEMENT
```

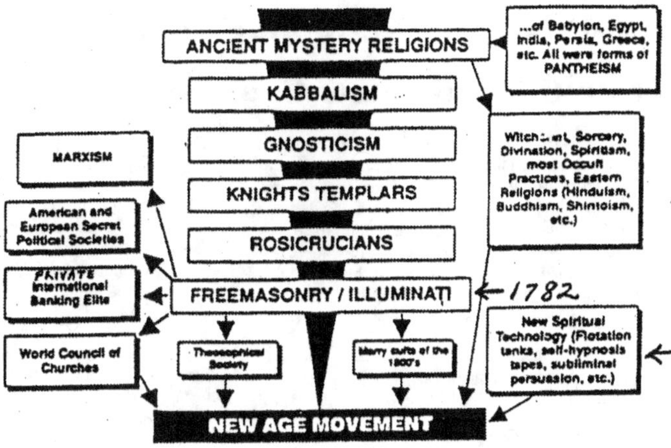

En Route to Global Occupation

Huntington House Publishers
P.O. Box 53788
Lafayette, Louisiana 70505

private *

▼ Federal Reserve Bank of New York stock includes twenty-seven New York
City banks. Listed below are the number of shares held by ten of these
banks

SECRETS OF THE FEDERAL RESERVE
The London Connection

Published by:
Bankers Research Institute
P.O. Box 1105
Staunton, VA 24401

	Shares	Percent
Bankers Trust Company	438,831	(6%)
Bank of New York	141,482	(2%)
Chase Manhattan Bank	1,011,862	(14%)
Chemical Bank	544,962	(8%)
Citibank	1,090,813	(15%)
✗ European American Bank & Trust	127,800	(2%)
✗ J. Henry Schroder Bank & Trust	37,493	(.5%)
Manufacturers Hanover	509,852	(7%)
Morgan Guaranty Trust	655,443	(9%)
✗ National Bank of North America	105,600	(2%)

It is notable that three of the banks holding Federal Reserve Bank of
New York stock, in the amount of 270,893 shares, are subsidiaries of foreign
banks. **(PRIVATE FOREIGN BANKS)**

Remove the FRB and the "national debt" disappears!

Not one cent of the so called income tax has ever been
applied to the national debt of the United States. All the
money collected by the IRS has gone straight to the Federal
Reserve System, a private banking owned monopoly.

On April 19, 1982, The case
was Lewis vs United States. The Ninth Circuit Court said,
"The Federal Reserve banks are privately owned, locally
controlled, seperate corporations, having absolutely nothing
to do with the Federal Government of the United States of
America."

The fact that the Federal Reserve Board regulates the
Reserve banks does not make them federal agencies under
the Act. (H.R. Report No. 69, 63 Cong. lst Sess. 18-19
(1913)

SENATOR HENRY BELLMON OF OK-
LAHOMA—testifying before the Finance Committee October 2, 1969 said: "In a recent
conversation with an official at the Internal Revenue Service, I was amazed
when he told me that, 'If the taxpayers
of this country ever discover that the Internal Revenue Service operates on
90% bluff, the entire system will collapse.'"

LET'S FIX IT!

America created its own money in 1750

How Benjamin Franklin made New England prosperous

The following historical story is taken from a radio-address given by Congressman Charles G. Binderup, of Nebraska, about 50 years ago (reprinted in "Unrobing the Ghosts of Wall Street).

By Charles G. Binderup

Colonies more prosperous
Than the home country

Before the American War for Independence (1776), the colonized part of what is today the united States of America was a possession of England. It was called New England, and was made up of 13 colonies, which became the first 13 States of the great Republic.

Around 1750, this New England was very prosperous. Benjamin Franklin was able to write:

"There was abundance in the Colonies, and peace was reigning on every border. It was difficult, and even impossible, to find a happier and more prosperous nation on all the surface of the globe. Comfort was prevailing in every home. The people, in general, kept the highest moral standards, and education was widely spread."

When Benjamin Franklin went over to England to represent the interests of the Colonies, he saw a completely different situation: the working population of this country was gnawed by hunger and poverty. *"The streets are covered with beggars and tramps,"* he wrote. He asked his English friends how England, with all its wealth, could have so much poverty among its working classes.

His friends replied that England was a prey to a terrible condition: it had too many workers! The rich said they were already overburdened with taxes, and could not pay more to relieve the needs and poverty of this mass of workers. Several rich Englishmen of that time actually believed, along with Malthus, that wars and plague were necessary to rid the country from man-power surpluses.

Franklin's friends then asked him how the American Colonies managed to collect enough money to support their poorhouses, and how they could overcome this plague of pauperism. Franklin replied:

"We have no poorhouses in the Colonies; and if we had some, there would be nobody to put in them, since there is, in the Colonies, not a single unemployed person, neither beggars nor tramps."

Thanks to free money
Issued by the nation

His friends could not believe their ears, and even less understand this fact, since when the English poorhouses and jails became too cluttered, England shipped there poor wretches and down-and-outs, like cattle, and discharged, on the quays of the Colonies, those who had survived the poverty, dirtiness and privations of the journey. At that time, England was throwing into jail those who could not pay their debts.

They therefore asked Franklin how he could explain the remarkable prosperity of the New England Colonies. Franklin replied:

"That is simple. In the Colonies, we issue our own paper money. It is called 'Colonial Scrip'. We issue it in proper proportion to make the goods pass easily from the producers to the consumers. In this manner, creating ourselves our own paper money, we control its purchasing power and we have no interest to pay to no one."

The Bankers impose poverty

This information came to the knowledge of the English Bankers, and held their attention. They immediately took the necessary steps to have the British Parliament pass a law that prohibited the Colonies from using their scrip money, and then ordered them to use only the gold and silver money that was provided in insufficient quantity by the English Bankers. Then began in America the plague of debt-money, which has ever since brought so many curses to the American people.

The first law was passed in 1751, and then completed by a more restrictive law in 1763.

Franklin reported that one year after the implementation of this prohibition on Colonial money, the streets of the Colonies were filled with unemployed and beggars, just like in England, because there was not enough money to pay for the goods and work. The circulating medium of exchange had been reduced by half.

Franklin added that this was the original cause of the American Revolution – and not the tax on tea nor the Stamp Act, as it has been taught again and again in history books. The Financiers always manage to have removed from school books all that can throw light on their own schemes, and damage the glow that protects their power.

Franklin, who was one of the chief architects of the American independence, wrote it clearly:

"The Colonies would gladly have borne the little tax on tea and other matters had it not been the poverty caused by the bad influence of the English Bankers on the Parliament, which has

caused in the Colonies hatred of England and the Revolutionary War."

This point of view of Franklin was confirmed by great statesmen of his era: John Adams, Jefferson, and several others. A remarkable English historian, John Twells, wrote, speaking of the money of the Colonies, the Colonial Scrip:

"It was the monetary system under which America's Colonies flourished to such an extent that Edmund Burke was able to write about them: 'Nothing in the history of the world resembles their progress. It was a sound and beneficial system, and its effects led to the happiness of the people.'"

John Twells adds:

"In a bad hour, the British Parliament took away from America its representative money, forbade any further issue of bills of credit, these bills ceasing to be legal tender, and ordered that all taxes should be paid in coins. Consider now the consequences: this restriction of the medium of exchange paralyzed all the industrial energies of the people. Ruin took place in these once flourishing Colonies; most rigorous distress visited every family and every business, discontent became desperation, and reached a point to use the words of Dr. Johnson, when human nature rises up and asserts its rights."

Another writer, Peter Cooper, expresses himself along the same lines. After having said how Franklin had explained to the London Parliament the cause of the prosperity of the Colonies, he wrote:

"After Franklin gave explanations on the true cause of the prosperity of the Colonies, the Parliament enacted laws forbidding the use of this money in the payment of taxes. This decision brought so many drawbacks and so much poverty to the people that it was the main cause of the Revolution. The suppression of the Colonial money was a much more important reason for the general uprising than the Tea and Stamp Act."

Charles G. Binderup

* * *

The scrip of the Bankers

Today, in America as well as in Europe, we are under the regime of the Scrip of the Bankers instead of the scrip of the nation. Hence the public debts, everlasting interest charges, taxes that plunder purchasing power, with the only result being a consolidation of the financial dictatorship.

OPEN LETTER

President
White House
Washington, D.C. 20500 FAX, (202) 456-2461

Dear Mr. President:

Your first concern is the deficit? It is the usury,* now called interest, on the accumulated deficits that is hemorrhaging the economic life blood from the nation. There could be no such usury under Article 1, Sec. 8, Para. 5 of the Constitution if instead of the Federal Reserve, the country had a constitutional (usury-free) money system.

Your second concern is the "national debt" – in quotes because the $4 trillion is mostly fraud from pyramiding usury upon compounded usury. The actual deficits total but a fraction of that.

● Both of your concerns are caused by the <u>secret class A stockholders</u>** of the untaxed, unaudited Fed who number now with heirs 300; and some are American! They are the most avariciously predatory parasites upon a body politic in world history. The national bonded indebtedness is heavily held by the Fed. The process by which it acquires our bonds is not beyond understanding, but it is beyond belief. And why should the Treasury pay usury on bonds held by the Fed that our government has paid for – like a family squandering mortgage payments on a paid-up mortgage that should have been burned?

● Mr. President, you have the power to <u>buy back</u> the private central bank for <u>one half billion</u> dollars. You can issue the funds by Executive Order as did President <u>Kennedy</u> issue constitutional U.S. Notes and without congressional advice and consent. The class A stockholders capitalized their Fed with but $147 million, and after 80 years of racketeering now own America because they hold the mortgage!

There is the President <u>Lincoln</u> precedent – exactly 100 years prior to the Kennedy constitutional money: $364 million were issued usury-free at a time when the money mafia charged usury at the juice-loan rate of from 24% to 36%. Lincoln has saved us one half trillion dollars from being added to the "national debt". Only coinage is legal usury-free constitutional money. The "cashless society" is the bankers' coup de grace.

● Sec. 30 of the <u>Fed charter</u> offers you the option of <u>buying back</u> the Fed – as <u>confirmed</u> in <u>1927</u>, <u>1966</u> and <u>now</u>. The nation's life blood hemorrhaging out to usury would reverse back into the Treasury – the new Fed owner. Class B and C stock could remain unchanged. The income tax wasted on usury is now 84%, in '94 92%, and in '95 103%. It is too late to jump-start the economy. <u>Only</u> the buy-back of the Fed will rocket-blast the economy off the recession pad – while cutting taxes. Mr. President, you have the means and the match.

Respectfully,
George Edward Hiscott IV   LET'S FIX IT!
Life Member, Association of Former Intelligence Officers.

*   Historically a punishable crime until 1694.
** Warburg Bank of Hamburg and Amsterdam, Chase Manhattan Bank of New York, Rothschild Banks of London and Berlin, Goldman Sachs Bank of New York, Lazard Brothers Bank of Paris, Kuhn Loeb Bank of New York, Israel Moses Sief Banks of Italy, Lehman Brothers Bank of New York
All reprint rights granted

On June 8, 1993, the Chairman of the House Committee on banking, Henry Gonzales (D-Texas), warned the nation in a speech condemning the "Fed" by saying, "All history shows that no society has been able to endure usury."

<u>ABOLISH</u> THE
FEDERAL RESERVE BANK, "<u>THE FED</u>,"
AND THE INTERNAL REVENUE SERVICE, "<u>IRS</u>"

19

"War is just a racket." 2

Major General S. Butler, US Army <u>BREAKS THE CODE OF SILENCE</u>! "War is just a racket. A racket is best described, I believe, as something that is NOT what it seems to the majority of the people. Only a small 'insider group' knows what it is about. It is conducted for the benefit (profit) of the 'very few' at the expense (destruction) of the masses (people).

"The trouble with America is that when the dollar only earns 6 % interest (usury) over here [to pay 'war bonds' from previously funded 'wars'], then it (the dollar) gets restless and goes overseas to get 100 %. Then, the 'flag' follows the 'dollar' and the soldiers follow the flag. This is done to 'defend' some lousy (rotten) 'investment' of the (private international) bankers.

"There isn't a trick in the 'racketeering bag' that the 'military gang' is blind to. It has its 'finger men' to point out enemies, its 'muscle men' to destroy enemies, its 'brain men' to plan war preparations, and a 'BIG BOSS' – supernationalist capitalism, (meaning THEFT by men and women who own the previous 'wars' bonds or, better said, the speculators).

"I spent most of my life being a 'high muscle man' for big business ('war' speculators), for Wall Street and for the (private) bankers. In short, I was a 'racketeer', a gangster for (supernationalist) capitalism.

"I helped make Mexico, and especially Tampico, safe for 'American' oil interests in 1914. I helped make Haiti and Cuba a 'decent place' for the 'National City (private) Bank boys', to collect revenues (taxes) in. I helped in the 'raping' of half a dozen Central American republics for the benefit of Wall Street.

"The record of 'racketeering is long. I helped 'purify' Nicaragua for the (private) international banking house of Brown Brothers in 1908-1912. I brought 'light' to the Dominican Republic for 'American sugar interests in 1916. In China, in 1927, I helped to 'see to it' that Standard Oil went its way 'unmolested.'

[ED: From General Butler's 1933 Armistice Day speech in Philadelphia, Penna. as cited in the 1982 book; <u>Wealth for All Religion, Politics and War</u>, pages 210 & 211, by R.E. McMaster.

"When commerce begins to wane, and profits are low, 'wars' are fought to create or protect 'markets' for the 'speculators,' who OWN governments through funding 'systems', (such as today's Federal Reserve [private] Banks, "FRB"; the [private] International Monetary Fund, "IMF" the IMF is the [private] bank for the United Nations, "U.N." as well as the [private] World Bank).

"Their 'funding systems' and (their) taxing 'power' is nothing more than (PRE-planned) imposed SLAVERY Now, (a caution and warning), from the New Testament of the Holy Bible, the book of James, chapter 4, verses 1 – 3,: "From whence come wars and fighting among you? Come they not hence, even of your lusts that war in your members? Ye lust, and have not: ye kill and desire to have, and cannot obtain: ye fight and war, yet ye have not, because you ask not. Ye ask, and receive not, because ye ask amiss, that ye may consume it upon your lusts."

UNITED STATES NOTE

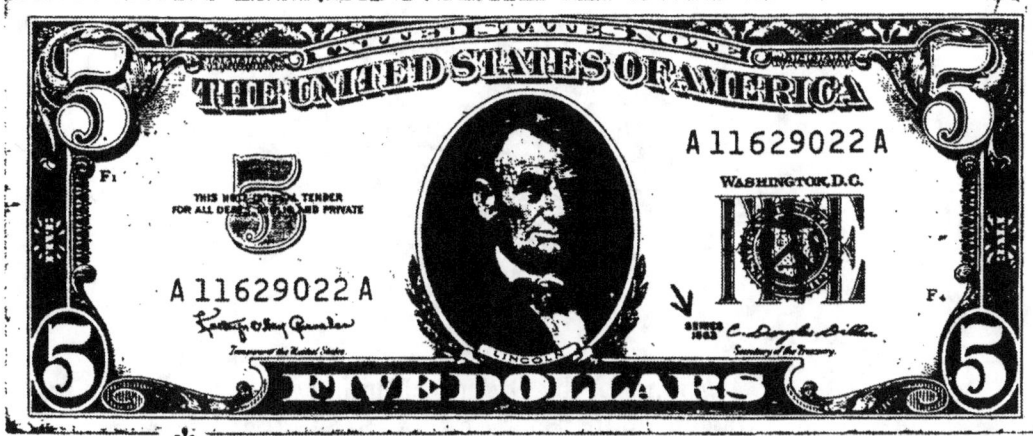

* Proper Constitutional money, gold & silver backed, (United States Notes) or (Lincoln greenbacks), makes the economy SING - this is why the international private bankers also murdered Lincoln !

35th PRESIDENT

LIVED AFTER TERM .Died in office
DATE OF DEATH Nov. 22, 1963
AGE AT DEATH 46 years, 177 days
PLACE OF DEATH Dallas. Tex.

* ESTABLISH DEBT FREE CONSTITUTIONAL CURREN-CY AND ELIMINATE THE FED. immediately reinstate the JFK Executive Order authorizing the printing of $450 billion in no interest "United States Notes." This will put the privately owned banking consortium known as the Federal Reserve System out of business until the public can be informed of its insidious role in our current economic crisis. Congress can then be made to return to Con-stitutional currency. It makes no sense to pay usury on our own money. Federal Reserve banks use the national debt as collateral and through "fractionalized banking," lend many times that amount at interest back to the people. Since assuming the Congressional responsibility for legal tender in 1913, the FED has never been audited! Thomas Jef-ferson warned us if ever the banks took over our currency and credit, our children would wake up as slaves on the continent conquered by their fathers!

<u>DEMAND</u> AN AUDIT OF THE FRB BANKS !

SEE EXECUTIVE ORDER #11110. 4 June 1963

THE FIRST ACT OF BUSINESS CONDUCTED BY PRESIDENT JOHNSON FOLLOWING JFKs DEATH WAS TO CANCEL THE 450 BILLION IN U.S. NOTES !

* CONSTITUTIONAL MONEY MAKES THE ECONOMY ROAR !

Insignia of the Order of Illuminati
Appears on the Back of All U.S. $1.00's

The above insignia of the Order of the Illuminati was adopted by Adam Weishaupt at the time he founded the Order on May 1, 1776. It is that event memorialized by the MDCCLXXVI at the base of the pyramid, and not the date of the historic signing of the Declaration of Independence, as the uninformed have supposed.

The significance of the design is as follows: "The pyramid represents the conspiracy for the destruction of Christianity and the establishment of a "One World" dictatorship under Satanic despotism, this being the *secret* of the Order; the radiating in all directions – the "all-spying" eye represents the "Big Brother," or terroristic all-knowing espionage agency that Weishaupt set up under the name of "Insinuating Brethren," to guard the secret of the Order and to terrorize the populace into acceptance of its rule. "Annuit Coeptis" means *our enterprise* (conspiracy) and has been crowned with unbelievable success. "Novus Ordo Seclorum" explains the nature of the enterprise and it means "*a new social order*" or "New Deal."

This seal acquired Freemasonry significance only after the merger of that Order with the Order of the Illuminati at the Congress of Wilhelmsbad, in 1782.

This seal first appeared on the back of the U.S. dollar bill at the beginning of the New Deal, 1933, by order of President Franklin D. Roosevelt. Evidently, with the advent of his New Deal, the Illuminists regarded their efforts as a beginning which was being crowned with success. In effect, this seal proclaims to the One Worlders that the entire power of the United States Government is now controlled by the agentur of the Illuminati and is persuaded, or forced, to adopt policies which further the secret plans of the conspirators (Gadiantons) to undermine and destroy it altogether, with the remaining governments of the so-called "Free World." This includes freedom of speech, assembly, religion, free market system, etc., including all Rights reserved under the "Bill of Rights."

JFK AND THE FED

President John F. Kennedy was the last president to defy the Federal Reserve - and look what happened to him. Kennedy was a maverick who often acted independently, and at times in direct conflict with the agendas of many Powerful Washington Special Interests. One of these powerful Special Interests was the Federal Reserve.

Economist Seymour Harris described Kennedy as *"by far the most knowledgeable president of all time in the general area of economics. "* President George W. Bush, to bolster his tax-cut proposal, accurately demonstrated how Kennedy, in 1961, passed a much larger tax cut than the one he implemented. At the time, Kennedy articulated a profound understanding of the economic principle of leaving the maximum amount of capital at the source of production, with the taxpayer. Most economists agree that the Kennedy tax cut contributed greatly to the prosperous economy of the 1960. And President Reagan's 1981 tax cut contributed to the prosperity of the '80s and '90s.

With regard to the Fed, James J. Saxon, Kennedy's comptroller of currency, encouraged a policy of broader investment and lending powers to be granted to non-Fed-affiliated banks. This would involve allowing for the setting of interest rates by these independent banks and lenders that could compete with those set by the Fed and its affiliates. Saxon also decided that these non-Fed banks and institutions could underwrite state and local bond issues, an area that had been bailiwick for the Fed-affiliated banks. These policies set Kennedy at odds with the powerful central banking system.

In June 1963, President Kennedy authorized the issuance of more than $4 billion in debt-free *"United States Notes"* instead of "Federal Reserve Notes" through the US Treasury. This extraordinary act completely circumvented the unconstitutional Federal Reserve, which expects to be called upon to lend currency to the US Government, at interest accruing to themselves. Kennedy tried to reduce the national debt by avoiding the paying of interest to the *privately owned nonfederal* Federal Reserve.

The last time a president did this was in 1862, when Abraham Lincoln authorized the issuance of $450 million in debt-free currency known at the time as "greenbacks" - through the US Treasury, rather than borrowing money from the banking establishment. Lincoln stated:
"Government possessing power to create and issue currency - need not and should not borrow capital at interest. The privilege of creating and issuing money is not only the supreme prerogative of the government, but is the government's greatest creative opportunity."

Is it just a coincident that both Presidents Abraham Lincoln and John F. Kennedy were assassinated? Kennedy opposed many powerful interests during his all-too-brief presidency, not the least of whom were those in his own government, such as the likes of McNamara, Rusk, the Bundy brothers, etc., who were clamoring for war in Vietnam.

The widow of accused assassin Lee Harvey Oswald, in a 1994 interview with author A. J. Weberman, said: *"The answer to the Kennedy assassination is with the Federal Reserve Bank. Don't underestimate that. It's wrong to just blame the CIA. This is only one finger of the same hand. The people who supply the money are above the CIA. "*

SCOOPIFIED
P.O. Box 277
Bellingham, W A 98227

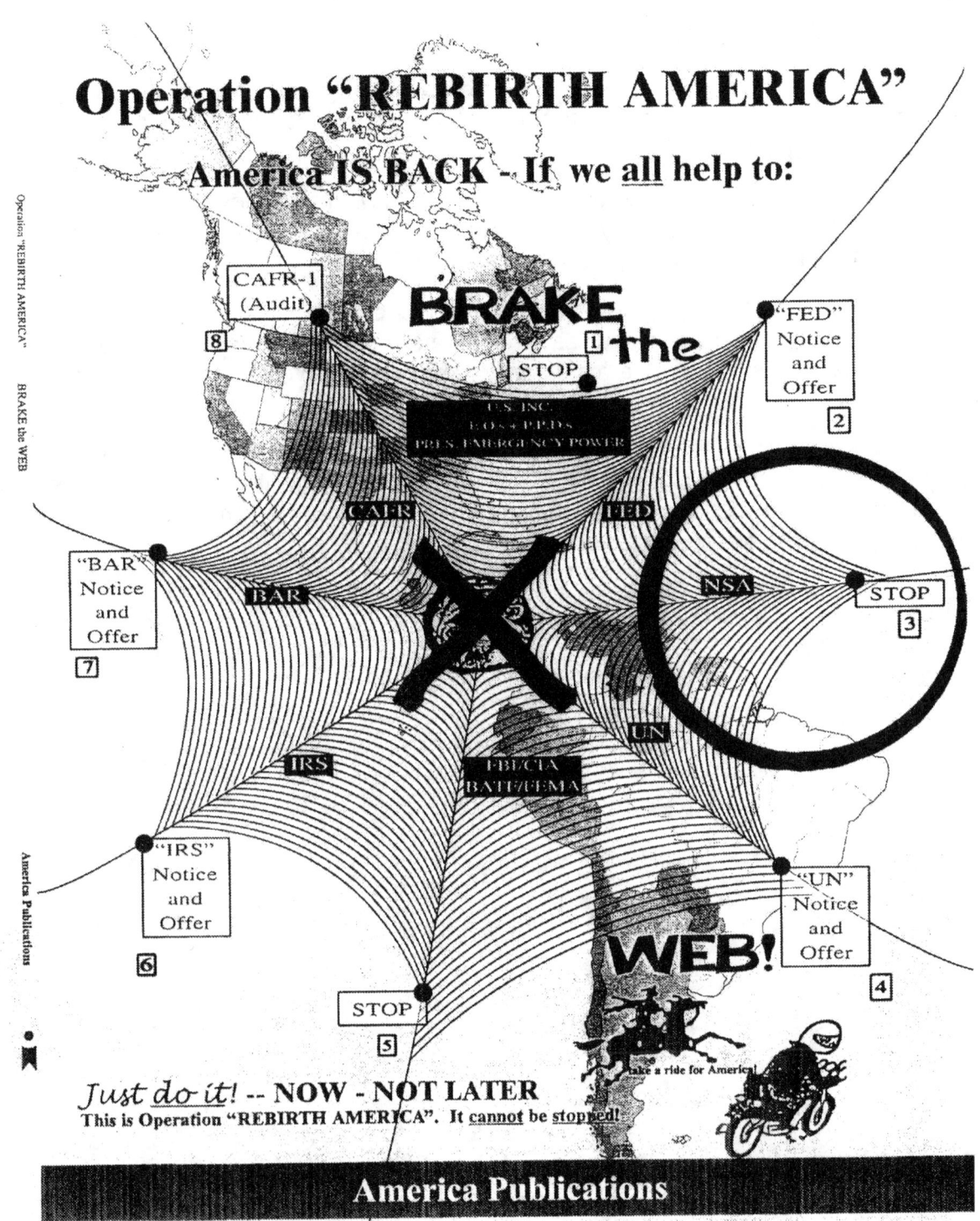

Operation "REBIRTH AMERICA"

America IS BACK - If we all help to:

BRAKE the **WEB!**

Take a ride for America!

Just do it! -- NOW - NOT LATER
This is Operation "REBIRTH AMERICA". It cannot be stopped!

America Publications

What is a "Black Project"?

A "Black Project" is:

1. A higher than top secret project funded by unknown individuals and governments, (governments approve money but never know where the money goes, what it is used for and never get it back).

2. A above top secret power group controls how the money is used. They coordinate construction of, lets say, a "flying saucer", (see #3 below), or the above top secret conditioning of controlled agents, (see #4 below).

3. The accomplishments are made by keeping each small part manufactured at different locations (by separate companies) or separate, above top secret departments. These parts are then assembled at a completely separate, above top secret location by totally controlled individuals.

4. "Black Project" Agents are above top secret and have been through up to 5 levels of "Open Eyes" brainwashing. This is accomplished through the use of hypnosis and drugs. The agent will respond to trigger words, pleasing only his "employer" and following ALL instructions, including assassinations.

THE INTELLIGENCE EXAMINER

Investigative Report
1708 Patterson Road
Austin, Texas 78733-6507

WORLD SURVEILLANCE HEADQUARTERS
DARK SECRETS OF THE NATIONAL SECURITY AGENCY

The *National Security Agency (NSA)* is the most dangerous, most secretive organization on planet Earth. One reliable intelligence source identifies this super-sleuth, police state agency as "World Surveillance Headquarters." Yet, surprisingly, only a handful of people are even aware of its existence.

The NSA employs thousands of government bureaucrats, intelligence officials, military personnel, and technological specialists in a global-wide operation. Its headquarters—closely guarded by U.S. Army security personnel at Fort Meade, Maryland—is housed in

A rare photo of the heavily guarded National Security Agency (NSA) complex at Fort Meade, Maryland.

the second largest building in the United States, surpassed only by the Pentagon in Washington, D.C. This huge, behemoth of a facility, appropriately enough, has been called the "Puzzle Palace."

The mission of the NSA, broad and all-encompassing, involves war planning, security investigations, classified materials control, and management of America's far-flung spy and intelligence network. The CIA, the State Department, even the White House and its occupants, take orders from the unseen chiefs at the NSA.

The infamous activities and international crimes of France's intelligence service, Russia's KGB secret police, Israel's spy agency, the Mossad, Britain's MI-6, and Canada's Secret Intelligence Service (CSIS) can all be laid at the feet of America's notoriously evil National Security Agency.

The whirring of the computers and the eerie sounds emanating from the ultra-classified, cryptographic machines inside the NSA's Puzzle Palace never cease. Twenty-four hours a day, the NSA hums along, its giant computer network correlating, deciphering, and analyzing data and reports from spy satellites, from remote telephone wiretaps and sensors, from international banks, from the 32 directorates of the United Nations, and from the bowels of the Secret Societies, the Vatican curia,

and the various agencies of over 170 nations around the globe.

This hulking monstrosity is the fount of global evil for the New World Order, which some now euphemistically call the "New Civilization." It is responsible for genocidal massacres of hundreds of thousands of people in Rwanda, Burundi, and Angola in Africa, for the brutal ethnic cleansing and killing camps in Bosnia, and for the bloody, experimental concentration camp operation run by NSA stooge Jim Jones of the Peoples Temple, in Guyana, South America.

The National Security Agency is guilty of horrific, murderous, and barbaric acts of terrorism everywhere on planet Earth. With their so-called "black budgets," the NSA and its inferior organizations sponsor, create, fund, and manage terror units and groups of all ideological stripes and shades.

But the chief and most strategic mission of the labyrinth known as the National Security Agency is the development, construction, and oversight of the Beast 666 Universal Human Control System.

Through its supervision of the *Defense Advanced Research Projects Agency (DARPA)* the NSA has been able to create and install a fabulous, global system of computers, satellites, telecommunications devices, and surveillance gadgetry. The men who plot behind the massive, locked doors of the NSA's Puzzle Palace have also spent as much as $250 billion dollars—spread over the past quarter of a century—to create fantastic, high tech systems of human control.

As you will discover in this mind-boggling, audiotaped investigative exposé, these systems of control are so diabolically effective that only a mastermind could originally have conceived them. Can there really be any doubt about it? Is the Chief Executive Officer of the NSA a human being...or is this monstrous agency headed behind the scenes by Lucifer himself?

60 Minute Audiotape — For Your Gift of $10

The NSA was established by implication, as was the FBI,BATF, the CIA, et al. NO law in the Constitution and Bill of Rights is by implication, therefore all of these agencies have no mandate and are unlawful agencies. NONE of the foregoing is EXPRESSLY IMPLIED in the delegated powers of government, Article 1,Sec.8,Clauses 1-18. Therefore, the agencies mentioned above, and most likely many others, are INHIBITED or PROHIBITED by the Constitution. This was confirmed by Chief Justice John Marshall: "When the Constitution is SILENT on a power, it is a PROHIBITION of that power."

1708 Patterson Road, Austin, Texas 78733

THE INTELLIGENCE EXAMINER

Investigative Report by Texe Marrs

WE, ROBOTS: Slavery and Contentment in the Age of Big Brotherism

In the 1940's the United States concentrated the greatest scientific minds on earth and spent over a billion dollars on the Manhattan Project—the development of the first atomic nuclear bomb. The Top Secret project was a phenomenal success. In early August 1945, U.S. Army-Air Force planes demolished the Japanese cities of Hiroshima and Nagasaki, raining down atom bombs and effectively ending the Second World War.

Since Hiroshima, many trillions of dollars have been spent on other successful Top Secret government projects, with names like Moonstruck, MK-ULTRA, Orion, Trident, Tower, Milab, and HAARP. These billions have been spent not only on weapons that can destroy human bodies and decimate cities, but on an entirely different type of weapon. For over 50 years, the United States and a few others have been actively developing heinous weapons to silently enter an enemy's body and seize control of his mind and soul.

These monstrous, secret weapons of human control are now ready for immediate use against the newly designated enemy. You and I are that enemy!

In this shocking investigative report, Texe Marrs opens his confidential files to disclose the nature of these sinister new anti-human weapons and human control systems. He meticulously describes their operation and details how many are being employed now—or will be employed soon—against we, the designated enemy. He also reveals the astonishing, real objective of this dazzling and dizzying array of mind-warping and body-invasive new systems. That objective is nothing less than the bionic transformation of the whole human race into mind-controlled, remotely monitored robots.

In the New Age World prepared for us all—once we bridge the year 2000 and move forward into the next millennium—we shall be robots. Yes, even robot slaves, contented with our lot, all of us working and acting together in unison as one, giant integrated electronic mind—the 'Borg.' Then and only then will mankind be happy and compliant, hating and despising God Almighty in Heaven, while loving and yearning for the praises and approval of the gods ruling over us and through us. On that day, if the optimistic plans of the technocrats succeed, there will be only two classes, or species, of life on Earth: They, our Elitist Masters, and We, Robots.

Now, A Stunning Exposé of Human/Robot Conversion Technology:

~ Mind-reading machines, secretly developed by DARPA and top scientific researchers, which can interpret a person's brainwaves and reveal what that person is thinking—or has ever thought!

~ Holographic 3-D imagery, using advanced lasers, that can create colorful moving, talking, and acting images to simulate signs in the heavens, visions of angels and "light beings," UFOs, and even, someday soon, the image of the beast.

~ Electromagnetic and chemical "therapy" which creates false memories in the mind of alien abductions, men in black, and UFO visitations.

~ Microwave and ELF wave weapons that cause headaches, nausea, skin burns, fatigue, irritability, mental disease, premature aging, tissue deterioration, and cancer.

~ Harmonic resonance weapons that invade the minds of masses of people. They can induce anger and incite mobs to riot, loot, burn and kill. They can also create entire societies of "ideal citizens,"—happy, subservient, robotic slaves.

~ Brainwave generators that use computer-modulated series of flashing lightwaves sent over television screens to an unsuspecting mass audience. In one secret experiment in Japan, this device was used to emit flashing lights from the eyes of the main character of the popular children's cartoon show, "Pokemons." Immediately, hundreds of Japanese children watching the show in their homes were sent into violent convulsions, vomiting, and epileptic fits. Hundreds had to be hospitalized.

~ Echelon, a new and highly secret global surveillance system developed by America's National Security Agency, now in use monitoring all of the world's telephones, faxes and Internet e-mails.

~ A national DNA databank for all U.S. citizens, first disclosed in a Texe Marrs book and now admitted as a reality by the FBI.

~ A computerized "God module," hard-wired into the human brain, that induces mystical experiences and allows the person to know "God" and believe in the programmed religion.

~ Computer biochips implanted in the brain, arm, or hand, already tested and in use, enabling the individual to direct mechanical systems by thought—and allowing a remote controller to implant thoughts and instructions in the mind.

Mind Control Has No Limits

by Robert LeBeaux, Dec., 1998 A.D.

This special report will put citizens on notice that they can now be placed under 24-hour surveillance by any of the 50,000 operatives of the National Security Agency (NSA). What is the NSA? Let us start by stating what it is not: it is NOT a constitutional body; it is outside the pale and the ken of the U.S. Constitution and Bill of Rights as it is NOT mentioned in the Constitution nor is it an expressly implied power found in Part 1, Section 8, Clauses 1-18 of the U.S. Constitution.

As Chief Justice John Marshall--the first chief justice of the U.S. Supreme Court said: "The U.S. Constitution is an instrument of grants and inhibitions (prohibitions) of power and not a definition of which there is but one, treason, in Article 3, Section 3, Parts 1 & 2." The ONLY grant of power to the Federal Government is contained in Article I, Section 8, Clauses 1-18. As the NSA and the CIA are NOT in this grant of power, both are unconstitutional entities.

There are those in government who think they can create one government agency after another merely by the stroke of a pen, but this is not so. For the government to have such powers, would "render the Constitution a blank paper by construction" (Jefferson). The 10th Amendment fixes the type and limitations upon organic law, and makes the Federal Government one of delegated powers and not original powers. By creating the NSA and the CIA, government has taken original powers expressly forbidden it by the Constitution.

The NSA was established by implication, as was the FBI, BATF, the CIA, et al. NO law in the Constitution and Bill of Rights is by implication, therefore all of these agencies have no mandate and are unlawful agencies. NONE of the foregoing is EXPRESSLY IMPLIED in the delegated powers of government, Article 1, Sec. 8., Clauses 1-18. Therefore, the agencies mentioned above, and most likely many others, are INHIBITED or PROHIBITED by the Constitution. This was confirmed by Chief Justice John Marshall: "When the Constitution is SILENT on a power, it is a PROHIBITION of that power."

I think *we* have established as a constitutional fact that the NSA, like the CIA, has no constitutional mandate and in a strict interpretation of the Constitution, both operate as unlawful agencies of the federal government, in defiance of the will of the sovereigns of the nation, We, the People.

Yet, here we have the NSA, an agency established at Fort Meade, Maryland on par with the old KGB and probably 5 times the size of the KGB, ruling over the lives of We, the People. The so-called HUMINT (human intelligence agents) of the NSA are legion, probably even more than the 50,000 we know about. They have their "executive order" warrants: "Spy on any citizen who is of interest to *you.*" Of course this is not public knowledge, but the NSA has a massive surveillance apparatus in place for just this purpose, well disguised and hidden and if it is ever talked about, then it is under the cover of "anti-terrorism."

That's not all.

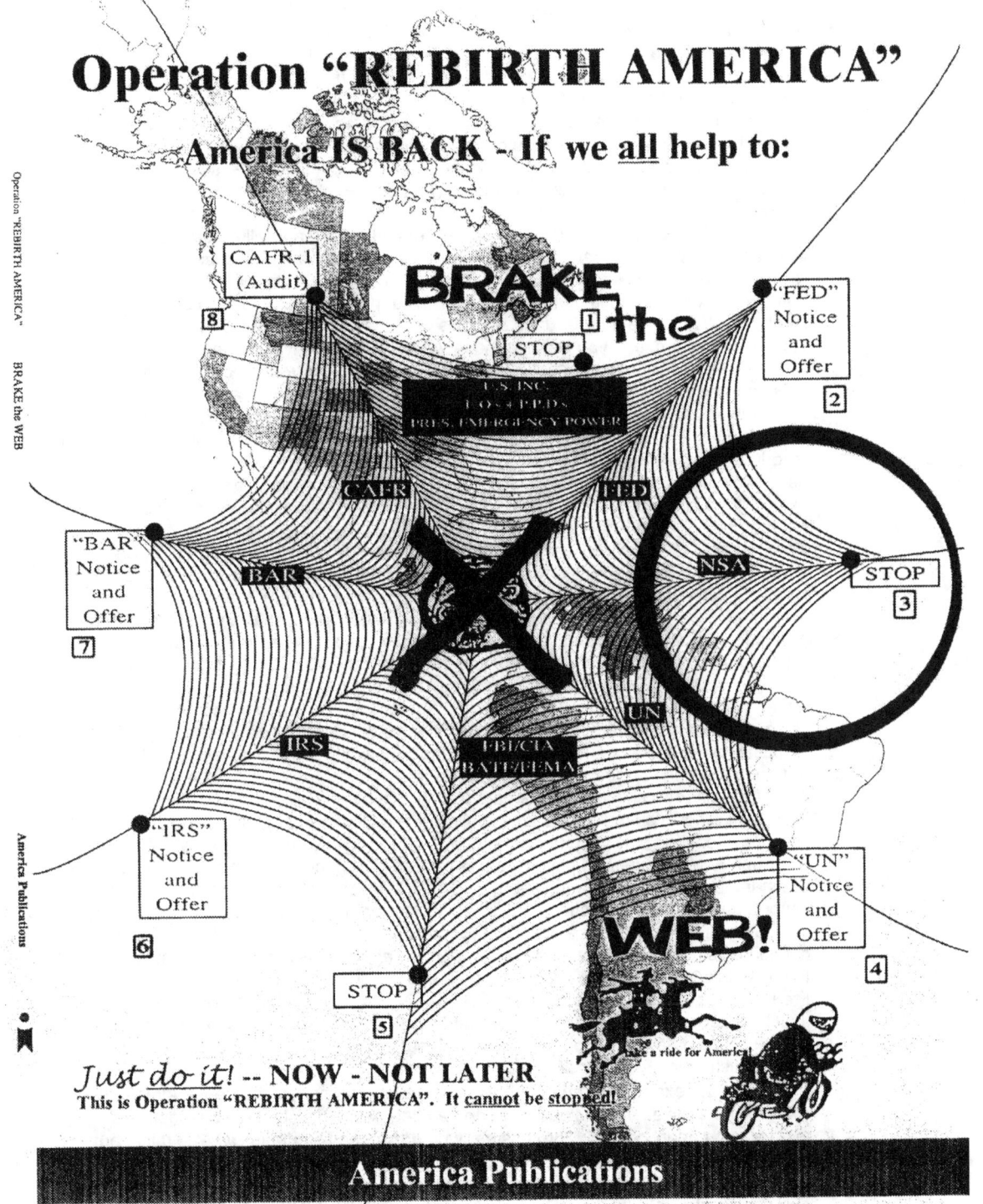

Operation "REBIRTH AMERICA"

America IS BACK - If we all help to:

Just do it! -- **NOW - NOT LATER**
This is Operation "REBIRTH AMERICA". It **cannot** be **stopped!**

TEACHING THE CHILDREN "WELL"

Dr. Chester Pierce is a Harvard Professor, Humanist and "New World Order" Guru. This professor instructs teachers and those students who aspire to become teachers of our children as follows: "Every child in America who enters school is mentally ill, because he or she comes to school with an allegiance to our institutions. Patriotism, nationalism and sovereignty, all that proves that children are sick because a truly well individual is one who rejects all of those things, and is truly the international child of the future."

Dr. Sidney Simon, lecturer and educator who some say specializes in encouraging immoral and criminal activity in youth. He instructs teachers as follows: 'We do not need more preaching about right and wrong. The old 'thou shalt nots' simply are not relevant. Values clarification is a method for teachers to change the values of children without getting caught."

American teachers now use a 'modern' version of 'humanist' literature to teach our children. One such book, entitled "Weep For Our Children", might explain why crime rates in school-aged children are skyrocketing. Consider this one passage touting the humanistic "Values Clarification / Situation Ethics" program: "It is OK to lie. It is OK to steal. It is OK to have promiscuous sex. It is OK to cheat and kill if these things are part of your value system, and you clarified these values for yourself. The important thing is not what values you choose, but that you have chosen them yourself freely and without coercion of parents, spouse, friends, minister, or social pressure of any kind."

This type of values & moral code (or lack thereof) is all too evident in our school system today. For decades, it has been the job of those within the field of psychology to introduce to the American public the idea that those who belief in God are sick and must be 'enlightened' or eliminated, and that immorality is the only path to the "New World Order". If you think that this change in the morals of our nation is accidental, you should read the book "The Soviet Art of Brainwashing - A Synthesis of the Russian Textbook on Psychopolitics", written by Kenneth Goff. In this book, Goff, a one-time dues-paying member of the Communist Party, writes: "During my training I was taught Psychopolitics, the art of capturing the minds of a nation through brainwashing and fake mental health." Kenneth Goff paid a high price for his effort to alert the American people of Marxist-trained psychologists being in place inside the U.S. He mysteriously died from poisoning in 1964. An excerpt from his book says: "This manual of the Communist Party should be in the hands of every loyal American, that they may be alerted to the fact that it is not always by armies and guns that a nation is conquered." In this book is found an address by Beria, the Head of the Lenin University School of Psychopolitics. His 1933 address to a group of Marxist Psychology students is most revealing. Speaking to a group who would be returning to ply their treachery in the U.S. he said:

"A psychopolitician must work hard to produce the maximum chaos in the fields of 'mental healing'. You must work until every teacher of psychology unknowingly or knowingly teaches only Communist doctrine under the guise of psychology. You musty labor until every doctor and psychiatrist is either a psychopolitician or an unwitting assistant to our goals. You must labor until we have domain over the minds of every important person in your nation (U.S.). You must work until suicide arising from mental imbalance is common and calls forth no general investigation or remark. You must dominate as respected men in the fields of psychiatry and psychology. You must dominate the hospitals and universities. You can take additional instructions as worshippers of Freud. With it you can erase our enemies like insects. Use the courts, use the judges, use the Constitution of the country, use the medical societies and its laws to further your ends. Create chaos. Leave a nation leaderless. Kill our enemies and bring to Earth, through Communism, the greatest peace man has ever known. Thank you."

This is an excerpt of Beria's speech to the visiting American students. Almost everything he asked these students to do has been accomplished. Our schools are teeming with "teachers" and "professors" who don't teach students *HOW* to think, but *WHAT* to think. Don't *YOU* think it's about time to cleanse our institutions of learning of this putrid "New World Order" infestation? Suggested Reading:

The Deliberate Dumbing Down of America, by Charlotte Thompson Iserbyt.

SCOOPIFIED
P.O.Box 277
Bellingham, W A 98227

Rumor has it that so many Americans have delivered the following
"Notice and Demand" to the United Nations that they are sick of hearing it.
(And so many have delivered it to our elected leaders that they have shut
down their toll-free phone numbers to avoid receiving it again.)

"The United Nations is the greatest fraud in all history. Its purpose is to destroy the United States." Congressman John E. Rankin

by America Publications Volunteers / 3370 North Hayden Road, # 148 / Scottsdale, Arizona 85251

Fax this to the White House – 1-202-456-2461
Fax this to the Senate – 1-202-224-2262
Fax this to the House of Representatives – 1-202-225-0697

Tell them to tell the United Nations:

"U.N., you are finished in America.
The U.S. is *out* of the U.N."

(Or, fax or tell this directly to the United Nations yourself.):

U.N. fax – 1-212-963-0071 / U.N. e-mail http://www.inquires@un.org
U.N. phone 1-212-963-4475 (or) 1-212-963-9246

(Also U.N. employees and others)

NOTICE AND OFFER

We Americans hereby <u>notify</u> you that we <u>offer</u> you, the United Nations, complete amnesty if you permanently vacate your offices in America for the following reasons:

- Your unlawful and illegal Charter/Treaty was saddled on America and other sovereign nations subversively and fraudulently 55 years ago.
- You have promoted secret, pre-planned disruptions and wars, using <u>mercenary</u>* soldiers from your "member" countries.
- Your secret slavery agenda is by design of ten un-elected 'leaders' who take orders from the private international banking cartel.
- Your so-called "Charter" with its secret agenda for a "one-world government" is totally and completely against our long-established Constitution for the united States, its <u>permanent</u> Bill of Rights, our Declaration of Independence, and our associated traditions of liberty.
- NOW THEREFORE, WE <u>NOTIFY</u> YOU THAT WE <u>OFFER</u> YOU COMPLETE AMNESTY IF YOU CLOSE YOUR OPERATIONS IN THE UNITED STATES OF AMERICA –   AND LEAVE OUR COUNTRY WITH ALL DELIBERATE SPEED.

*<u>Mercenary</u> = a person in the service of an armed force not of his own nation – as, for example, a United Nations soldier – who is not protected by his own nation. Incidentally, mercenaries are not protected by the Geneva Convention, either.

America Publications Volunteers / 3370 North Hayden Road, # 148 / Scottsdale, Arizona 85251

The Governor of each State grants "AMNESTY".

Sample state Resolution *

* To immediately and permanently remove the CHARTER OF THE UNITED NATIONS TREATY and FLAG from the state of
_____.

Resolution

Whereas the CHARTER OF THE UNITED NATIONS TREATY with its FLAG is seriously flawed in that it allows a "select few" members to change, alter or repeal any article at their will in direct violation of _____ state law, and;

Whereas, the CHARTER OF THE UNITED NATIONS TREATY is in direct contradiction to the _____ state Constitution and the Constitution of the united States of America with its Bill of Rights in that it allows a "select few" members to change, alter, or repeal the Rights of the People which are unchangeable according to the Bill of Rights of the Constitution of the united States of America, and;

Whereas, the FLAG of the UNITED NATIONS grants jurisdiction wherever and whenever it is displayed;

Therefore, be it resolved that, upon a majority vote of the _____ House and Senate, the UNITED NATIONS FLAG and its CHARTER/TREATY will be immediately and permanently removed from _____.

Sample Constitutional Amendment*
(Similar Amendment Proposed by Senator John Bricker of Ohio in 1952)

Proposed Constitutional Amendment

Section 1. It is clear in Article VI, paragraph two of the Constitution of the united States of America, "…Treaties made, or which shall be made, under the Authority of the United States, shall be the supreme Law of the Land;…", that the original writers and generations since assumed treaties to be used as treaties of peace or treaties identifying state geographic boundaries.

Section 2. With this Amendment a provision of a treaty which conflicts with the Constitution of the United States of America will not be of any force or effect.

Section 3. With this Amendment a treaty will become effective as international in the United States of America only through legislation which would be valid in the absence of treaty.

Section 4. With this Amendment Congress will have power to regulate all executive agreements with any foreign power or international organization. All such agreements will be subject to the limitations imposed on treaties by this Amendment and will be retroactive to effect all past treaties and agreements when this Amendment is properly ratified by the states.

* Senator Brickers' proposed Amendment was not ratified. In the early 1950s people were not anxious to remove the CHARTER OF THE UNITED NATIONS TREATY as they hoped it would be the answer to world peace. Now that we have experienced the UNITED NATIONS and its CHARTER/TREATY causing worldwide conflict and strife while violating the rights of all people OF ALL AGES, which is also REPUGNANT to the Constitution of the united States of America, IT IS TIME TO REMOVE IT WITH THIS AMENDMENT and protect the Constitution from past and future foul play!

From web site – ftp://ftp.loc.gov/pub/thomas/c105/h1146.ih.txt

FILE h1146.ih
HR 1146 IH
105th CONGRESS
1st Session
To provide for complete withdrawal of the United States from the United Nations

IN THE HOUSE OF REPRESENTATIVES
March 20, 1997

Mr. PAUL introduced the following bill; which was referred to the Committee on International Relations

A BILL

To provide for complete withdrawal of the United States from the United Nations.
[Italic->] Be it enacted by the Senate and House of Representatives of the United States of America in Congress assembled, [<-Italic]

- SECTION 1. SHORT TITLE.
  This Act may be cited as the 'American Sovereignty Restoration Act of 1997'.
- SEC. 2. REPEAL OF UNITED NATIONS PARTICIPATION ACT.
  (a) REPEAL- The United Nations Participation Act of 1945 (Public Law 79-264) is repealed.
  (b) CLOSURE OF UNITED STATES MISSION TO UNITED NATIONS- Effective within 120 days after the date of the enactment of this Act, the United States Mission to the United Nations shall be closed. Any remaining functions of such office shall not be carried out.
  (c) NOTICE- The Secretary of State shall notify the United Nations of the withdrawal of the United States from the United Nations as of the date of the enactment of this Act.
- SEC. 3. REPEAL OF UNITED NATIONS HEADQUARTERS AGREEMENT ACT.
  (a) REPEAL- The United Nations Headquarters Agreement Act (Public Law 80-357) is repealed.
  (b) WITHDRAWAL- Effective on the date of the enactment of this Act, the United States withdraws from the agreement between the United States and the United Nations regarding the headquarters of the United Nations (signed at Lake Success, New York, on June 26, 1947, which was brought into effect by the United Nations Headquarters Agreement Act).
  (c) NOTICE- The Secretary of State shall notify the United Nations that the United States has unilaterally withdrawn from the agreement between the United States of America and the United Nations regarding the headquarters of the United Nations as of the date of the enactment of this Act.
- SEC. 4. UNITED STATES ASSESSED AND VOLUNTARY CONTRIBUTIONS TO THE UNITED NATIONS.
  (a) TERMINATION- No funds are authorized to be appropriated or otherwise made available for assessed or voluntary contributions of the United States to the United Nations.
  (b) APPLICATION- The provisions of this section shall apply to all agencies of the United Nations, including independent or voluntary agencies.
- SEC. 5. UNITED NATIONS PEACEKEEPING OPERATIONS.
  (a) TERMINATION- No funds are authorized to be appropriated or otherwise made available for any United States contribution to any United Nations military operation.
- (b) TERMINATIONS OF UNITED STATES PARTICIPATION IN UNITED NATIONS PEACEKEEPING OPERATIONS- No funds may be obligated or expended to support the participation of any member of the Armed Forces of the United States as part of any United Nations military or peacekeeping operation or force. No member of the Armed Forces of the United States may serve under the command of the United Nations.

36

- SEC. 6. WITHDRAWAL OF UNITED NATIONS PRESENCE IN FACILITIES OF THE GOVERNMENT OF THE UNITED STATES AND REPEAL OF DIPLOMATIC IMMUNITY.

  (a) WITHDRAWAL FROM UNITED STATES GOVERNMENT PROPERTY- The United Nations (including any affiliated agency of the United Nations) shall not occupy or use any property or facility of the United States Government.

  (b) DIPLOMATIC IMMUNITY- No officer or employee of the United Nations or any representative, officer, or employee of any mission to the United Nations of any foreign government shall be entitled to enjoy the privileges and immunities of the Vienna Convention on Diplomatic Relations of April 18, 1961, nor may any such privileges and immunities be extended to any such individual.

- SEC. 7. REPEAL OF UNITED NATIONS EDUCATIONAL, SCIENTIFIC, AND CULTURAL ORGANIZATION ACT.

  (a) REPEAL- The Act entitled 'An Act providing for membership and participation by the United States in the United Nations Educational, Scientific, and Cultural Organization, and authorizing an appropriation therefor' approved July 30, 1946 (Public Law 79-565) is repealed.

  (b) NOTICE- The Secretary of State shall notify the United Nations that the United States has withdrawn from membership in the United Nations Educational, Scientific, and Cultural Organization as of the date of the enactment of this Act.

- SEC. 8. REPEAL OF UNITED NATIONS ENVIRONMENT PROGRAM PARTICIPATIN ACT OF 1973.

  (a) REPEAL- The United Nations Environment Program Participation Act of 1973 is repealed.

  (b) NOTICE- The Secretary of State shall notify the United Nations that the United States has withdrawn from membership in the United Nations Environment Program Participation as of the date of the enactment of this Act.

This copy of HR1146 received from the following web site:
ftp://ftp.loc.gov/pub/thomas/c105/h1146.ih.txt

- Dr. Ron Paul
  House of Representatives
  Washington D.C. 20515

1-888-322-1414   Weekly Message

31 May 2000 A.D.

Take a ride for America!

(Pat Revere requests that this dreadful history about how we lost the war in Korea be printed in this issue of the RVP. Grapevine Publications / Box 45057 / Boise, Idaho 83711) *"The United Nations is the greatest fraud in all history. Its purpose is to destroy the United States." Congressman John E. Rankin*

The U.N. is not our friend!
Lieutenant Colonel "Bud" Farrell, U S Air Force, retired

When I was a young officer and jet fighter pilot flying missions in the Korean Conflict (unknowingly under the command of a Soviet General of the <u>United Nations</u> Security Council), I could never understand HOW THE ENEMY KNEW SO MUCH ABOUT US, as broadcast almost daily over the communist Pyongyang radio station in North Korea.

Our wives' names, childrens' names, Squadron Commander names, flight numbers, etc.! The North Koreans knew when we were coming, how many of us there were, what type of aircraft we were flying and even the targets we were to hit. Later I realized that the naval and ground forces suffered the same fate that we did, especially our Army and Marine infantry troops.

All of our military operations had to be forwarded by radio to the Soviet Commander of the <u>United Nations</u> Security Council at the <u>United Nations</u> Building, New York City, for approval before our forces went into action against the North Koreans and Red Chinese. The Soviet Commander of the <u>United Nations</u> Security Council delayed the battle plans until he used the radios in the <u>United Nations</u> Building in New York to relay all our "battle planning information" to Moscow, North Korea and Red China.

The enemy then contacted and relayed these same battle plans to their communist forces in the field. The enemy knew when to move from an area and when to attack our smaller fighting forces. They knew beforehand when we were coming and how many of us there were. They knew everything about us all the time – 24 hours a day!!!

I later found this same form of "treason" was used against our forces in the VietNam War. All information regarding "every battle plan in Vietnam" was given to the North Vietnamese, Soviets (Advisors), and Viet Cong Troops in the field DURING THE ENTIRE WAR. The enemy knew our every move at all times.

Our troops were led like sheep to the slaughter in both Korea and Viet Nam. Like blind fools we sent our combat plans to the enemy for approval.

There was a standing joke among us fighter pilots. "That Moscow had a file on each and every one of us." How little did we really know. Every mission, every movement was compromised! General Walt, former Commander of the Untied States Marine Corps, reflected upon this information in his book that was written in the early 1980's. This was never allowed to appear in any bookstore in the United States. During the Korean and Viet Nam conflicts, thousands of our fighting men were mentally and physically incapacitated <u>BECAUSE OF THIS TREASON</u>! To this day, the Soviets (or someone from one of their satellite countries) are the only ones who can command the <u>United Nations</u> "World Police Forces".

Each and every one of us that served in Korea or Viet Nam served under the total command of a Soviet General!

GENERAL DOUGLAS MAC ARTHUR SPEAKS

"I was worried by a series of directives from Washington (Truman) which were greatly decreasing the potential of my Air Force. First I was forbidden 'hot' pursuit of enemy planes that attacked our own. Manchuria and Siberia were sanctuaries for all enemy forces and for all enemy purposes, no matter what depredations or assault might come from there. Then I was denied the right to bomb the hydroelectric plants along the Yula River. The order was broadened to include every plant in North Korea, which was capable of furnishing electric power to Manchuria and Siberia. Most incomprehensible of all was the refusal to let me bomb the important supply center at Racin in North Korea. I felt that step-by-step my weapons were being taken away from me. That there was a major leak in intelligence was evident to everyone. General Walker continually complained to me that his operations were known to the enemy in advance through sources in Washington."

General MacArthur then referred to an official leaflet published in China by Chinese General Lin Piao. It read: "I would never have made the attack and risk men and military reputation if I had not been assured that Washington would restrain General MacArthur from taking adequate retaliatory measures against my lines of supply and communications."

Although General MacArthur was unjustly smeared by the Controlled Press after he was fired by Harry Truman, the American people admired him. After his return from Korea he was given the biggest ticker-tape parade in history on April 20th, 1950, in New York City.

General Jack Jumper, a general in Vietnam, also knew what was going on with the UN and had our fliers hit targets in Cambodia, particularly the Ho Chi Min Trail, all without knowledge of the UN. Too many supplies were coming in from the North and they were getting ready for another offensive. General Jumper put a stop to it in 1972. Consequently, General Jumper was also taken out of his position. With White House approval the UN put him in charge of the Personnel Division. J. Ruben Clark Jr., former Under-Secretary of State and Ambassador to Mexico, who was widely recognized as one of our nation's foremost international lawyers, stated on page 27 in the book entitled *The United Nations Today:* "Not only does the Charter Organization (United Nations) not prevent future wars, but it makes it practically certain that we shall have future wars!" General Lewis William Walt, former Commander of the United States Marine Corps, reflected upon this information in his biography, written in the early 1980s. The book was never permitted to appear in any bookstore in the United States. Congressman John E. Rankin: "The United Nations is the greatest fraud in all history. It's purpose is to destroy the United States!"

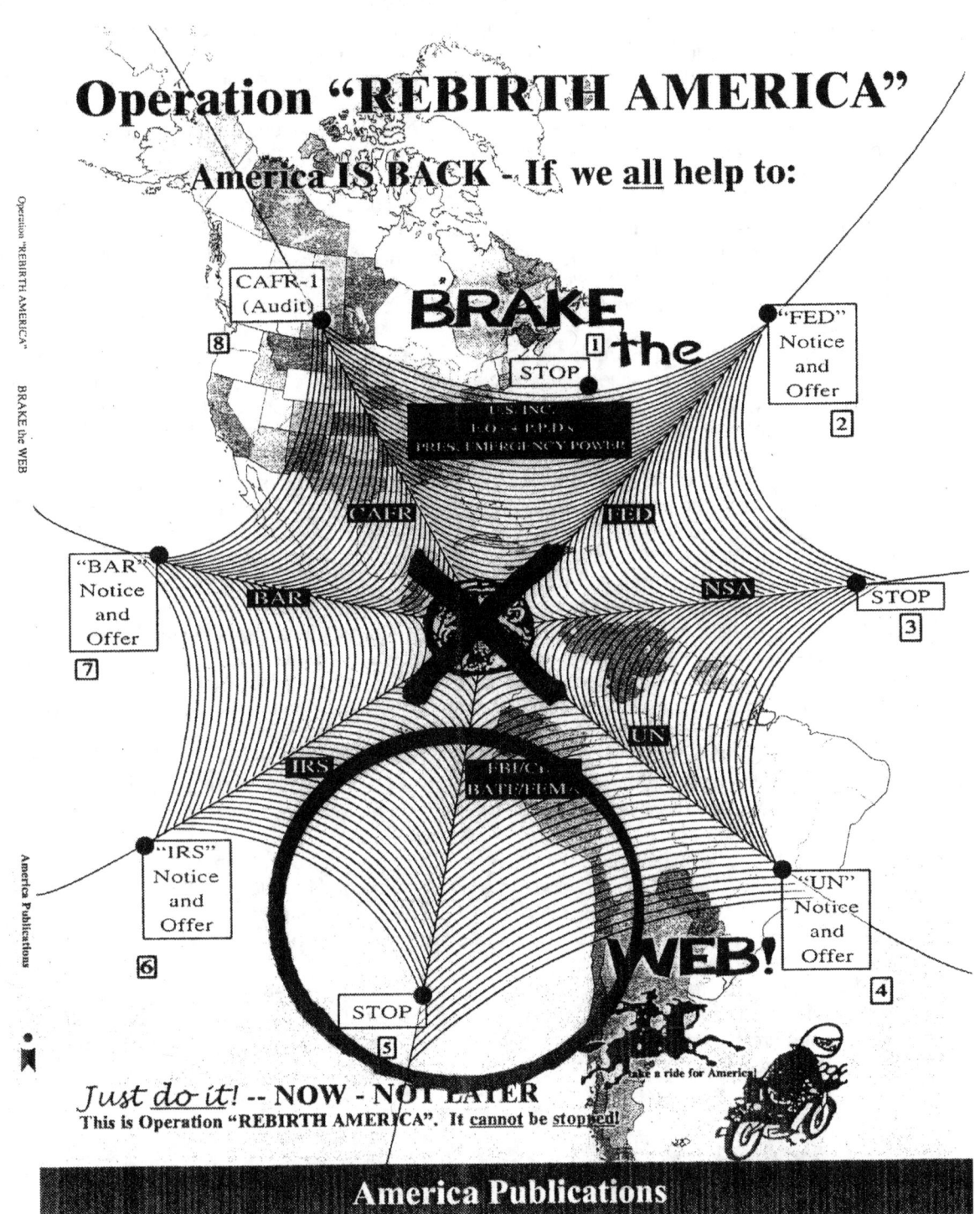

CHEMICALS AFFECTING BEHAVIOR AND HEALTH

Antisocial and criminal behavior has gone off the chart compared to just a short 50 years ago. 'Research by medical experts has proven that manmade poisons added to our food supply and environment are accumulating in our bodies thus playing a major role in this calamity. Scientists have accumulated evidence showing that most of current health and sociological miseries are the result of exposure to thousands of chemicals. Murder, rape, domestic violence, child abuse, school shootings, muggings, road rage, irritability, viciousness, diminished mental capacity, etc. have more so than ever - become part and parcel of American life. Cancer and dozens of other degenerative diseases are out of control.

We have been made to believe that crop yields need to be increased by the use of artificial fertilizers and pesticides; that household and garden products containing cocktails of chemicals are safe to use. We also fell for the fairy tale that chemical-laden processed foods are ok to eat. Finally, after decades of self-destruction, we begin to realize that we have been listening to the wrong people, people that have absolutely no concern for public well-being, but are only interested in their own financial gain.

James Carter, MD, points out in his book *"Racketeering in Medicine"* that agriculture now uses about 10 times as much pesticide and artificial fertilizer than 30 years ago, without significantly increasing the yield. Of the 70,000 chemicals currently in production, 3,000 have been added to our food supply. Hormone-polluted foods are causing men to grow breasts, and contribute heavily to the physical prematurity of our children.

Some 700 toxic chemicals can be found in our water supply. More than one third of all waterways are reported to be unsuitable for fishing or swimming. Typical sources of pollution include runoff from farms, industrial waste, and city sewer discharge. According to a report in *Newsweek*, millions of consumers are drinking tap water that is potentially hazardous due to chemical and bacterial contamination. The L.A. Times reported that communities with tap water contaminated by chemicals are being hit with strange patterns of illness. ABC Network News reported that U.S. industries generate some 88 million pounds of toxic waste a year, 90 percent of which - the E.PA estimates - are improperly disposed. The New York Times reported that more than 1 in 5 Americans drink tap water polluted with feces, radiation, chemicals, parasites and other contaminants. Some 1,000 death each year and at least 400,000 cases of waterborne illness may be contributed to water pollution.

With some 70,000 chemicals now in use and with the introduction of 1,000 more each year, tap water contamination is increasing at an alarming rate. Toxic chemicals are causing cancer, cell mutation, nervous disorders and a host of other diseases. Existing treatment plants are unable to remove this overload of toxins.

Neurotoxiology, a private Australian research group, reported that the widespread use of aluminum salts to 'purify' water may lead to brain damage and contribute to the Alzheimer's epidemic. Using aluminum to purify water may be even more dangerous than the use of fluoride and chlorine. It is believed that the problem is worsened by the action of fluoride in facilitating the absorption of aluminum.

Besides hazards for the unsuspecting general population, experts have noted the serious health consequences for the especially susceptible infants and children. Responsible citizens are left to educate and protect themselves from the world's greatest health threats - chemically contaminated food and water.

SCOOPIFIED
P.O.Box 277
Bellingham, W A 98227

STOP		FBI / CIA
		BATF /
		FEMA

The NSA was established by implication, as was the <u>FBI</u>, <u>BATF</u>, the <u>CIA</u>, <u>et al</u>. NO law in the Constitution and Bill of Rights is by implication, therefore all of these agencies have no mandate and <u>are unlawful agencies</u>. NONE of the foregoing is EXPRESSLY IMPLIED in the delegated powers of government, Article 1, Sec. 8, Clauses 1-18. Therefore, the agencies mentioned above, <u>and most likely many others</u>, are INHIBITED or <u>PROHIBITED</u> by the Constitution. This was confirmed by Chief Justice John Marshall: "When the Constitution is SILENT on a power, it is a PROHIBITION of that power." Including "Homeland Security" and the "Patriot Act."

Back in the days of the Amendment to the Constitution of the united States of America called "The Prohibition (of alcohol) Amendment, a strange thing happened. Before "Prohibition", many people in America had discovered their cars, trucks, tractors and other motors worked extremely well, and economically on (home brewed) alcohol. Alcohol is cheap when you learn to make it yourself.

The "Oil Barons" saw immediately this "home brewed" alcohol was their ONLY competition, and they had to STOP it, (thank you John D. Rockefeller & Co. for writing the "prohibition Amendment" for your bought-and-paid-for U. S. Congress and their "state ratifiers" of the Amendment). NOTE: When juries throughout America began acquitting "Moonshiners" left and right, the Amendment was repealed, but, not without the "Alcohol Tax Stamp", (making alcohol more expensive than gas), along with the retention of the UNCONSTITUTIONAL federal "private army" known today as the Bureau of Alcohol Tobacco and Fire Arms, <u>BATF</u>.

Could it be - - the Central Intelligence Agency, <u>CIA</u>, took over the "worldwide drug trade" about 50 years ago? (Thank you George Bush for allowing one of your "drug deals" with Panama's President Noriaga to be tape recorded back when you were head of the CIA). NOTE: When you see a "DRUG BUST" in "HEADLINE NEWS" it is a "PLANNED BUST" to keep their CIA DRUG CONTROL "game" out of sight! Ask a Drug Dealer if he/she is ever concerned about being used as a <u>CIA/FBI</u> "patsy" in a "set up BUST"? This is how the <u>CIA</u> controls drugs "from the field to the street".

CIA Methods Of Control, "M.O.C."
Revealed!
…"keep the people barefoot, broke,
anxious, exhausted and downtrodden."
…"(in) induced poverty."
…"(in) economic stress."

Dear Fellow Americans.

In the late '70's I enlisted in the Army. Eventually I passed through the 82nd Airborne Division at Ft. Bragg, North Carolina. There, I volunteered for Special Forces, was accepted for training, passed and was assigned to an A-team in one of the groups. At the time President Reagan had replaced President Carter, and activity was increasing. Nicaragua, Sudan, Afghanistan, Delta Force was getting firmly established. The CIA was pulling skilled NCO's and officers.

During this time I participated in things which Patriots might believe are recent corruptions of the Constitution. For instance, plainclothes surveillance of civilian citizens. These citizens were not known to have committed any crime and were never aware that they, their friends and family were being watched. Pictures and notes of travel routes, work places, and homes were recorded. Sometimes this information would be turned over to a hit team. These guys would work out the best method, time and place to take someone. Either take him out or snatch them (him). It was only practice - - practice right to the event. But, it was also conditioning us.

Another type of training, given at Smith Lake, Ft. Bragg was intensive weapons training on targets dressed as civilians, including women and priests. I believe it was further conditioning of us, to remove psychological inhibitions. This was a distant root to Waco.

Lastly, and most chillingly, was a class that I attended given by the CIA. We were not allowed to take notes. It didn't register at the time, but does now. The title of the course was Methods of Control, known as M.O.C. It was about how to control a population through economic stress. Production shortages of material goods, consumption of peoples free time (Sports, TV, Drug, Sex & Alcohol Addiction, etc.) or induced poverty. The key was (is) to keep people barefoot, broke, anxious, exhausted and downtrodden. Any way (Lawful or unLawful) would do. Sound familiar?

I write you this to inform you (and break the "CODE OF SILENCE"). Your publication is the best chance to save ourselves and restore our lost liberties. The evil depend on ignorance (the "dumbing down" of America). Through correspondence and shared knowledge we can lift the rock these serpents hide under. We're a good people, but this has been a long time coming (pre-planned "gradualism" for complete slavery control, worldwide - - including America) and we must resist as best we can.
Thank you, A Patriot (name withheld)

"Once let the barriers of the Constitution be removed, and the march of abuse will be onward and without bounds."

Justice Daniels, U.S. Sup. Ct. (1849)

4.

[Look around America, now you know why you see so much "planned poverty" and "poor" people - - possibly you and me? The Central Intelligence Agency, "CIA", has done a "good job" training "enforcement people", right here and in and other countries, to enslave the population for the benefit of a "select few" at the top. This is NOT the America that I "put my life on the line for!" Let's ALL get busy and correct this shameful GREED and Lawlessness! If you have any further information on the CIA's "MOC" coarse, (or other agencies who are using their "methods"), and will share this with our readers, please BREAK THE CODE OF SILENCE and drop us a note.]

Congressman Ron Paul
LETTER FOR THE REPAIR OF AMERICA
FALL 1998

* Weekly Phone Message Up-date, 1-888-322-1414 *

Dear Friend:

The other day, I made a huge "gáffe" on national TV: I told the truth about the crimes of the U.S. government. As you can imagine, the ceiling fell in, and a couple of walls too.

Congressmen are supposed to support the government, I was told. Oh, it's okay to criticize around the edges, but there are certain subjects a member of the House of Representatives is not supposed to bring up. But I touched the real "third-rail" of American politics, and the sparks sure flew.

I was interviewed on C-SPAN's morning "Washington Journal," and I used the opportunity, as I do all such media appearances, to point out how many of our liberties have been stolen by the federal government. We must take them back.

The Constitution, after all, has a <u>very</u> limited role for Washington, D.C. If we stuck to the Constitution as written, we would have: no federal meddling in our schools; no Federal Reserve; no U.S. membership in the UN; no gun control and no foreign aid.

We would have no welfare for big corporations, or the *"poor"*; no American troops in 100 foreign countries; no Nafta, Gatt, or "fast-track"; no arrogant federal judges usurping states rights; no attacks on private property; and no income tax.

We could get rid of most of the cabinet departments, most of the agencies, and most of the budget. The government would be small, frugal, and limited.

That system is called liberty. It's what the Founding Fathers gave us. Under liberty, we built the greatest, freest, most prosperous, most decent country on earth.

It's no coincidence that the monstrous growth of the federal government has been accompanied by a sickening decline in living standards and moral standards.

The feds want us to be hamsters on a treadmill--working hard, all day long, to pay high taxes, but otherwise entirely docile and controlled. The huge, expensive, and out-of-control leviathan that we call the federal government wants to run every single aspect of our lives.

Cong. Ron Paul - P.O. Box 1776, Lake Jackson, Texas 77566

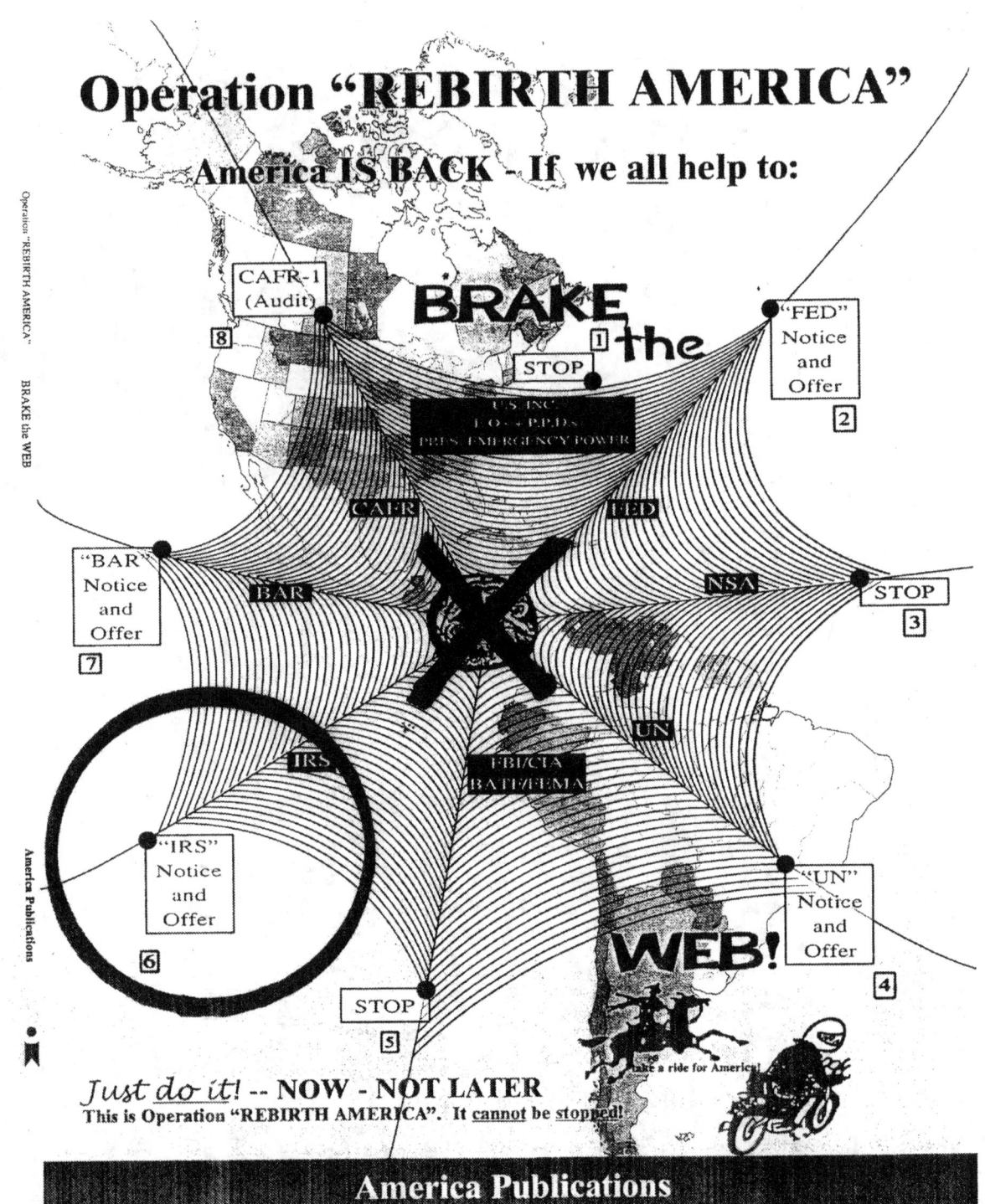

Operation "REBIRTH AMERICA"
America IS BACK - If we all help to:

BRAKE the WEB!

CAFR-1 (Audit) [8]

"FED" Notice and Offer [2]

"BAR" Notice and Offer [7]

STOP [3]

"IRS" Notice and Offer [6]

"UN" Notice and Offer [4]

STOP [5]

STOP [1]

Just do it! -- **NOW - NOT LATER**
This is Operation "REBIRTH AMERICA". It <u>cannot</u> be <u>stopped</u>!

Operation "REBIRTH AMERICA"   BRAKE the WEB   America Publications

America Publications

47

AFP on Taxes   AMERICAN FREE PRESS-645 Pennsylvania Avenue SE, Suite 100, Washington D.C. 20003   July 30, 2007 • AMERICAN FREE PRESS   7

www.americanfreepress.net

Jury Offers Major Victory to Tax Critics

By Peymon Mottahedeh

Attorney Tommy Cryer was found not guilty on all counts by a Louisiana jury in his landmark tax trial. Cryer is shown here at a Free Enterprise Society conference. The jury agreed with Cryer that he did not believe he had to pay taxes.

Lawyer Tommy K. Cryer was found not guilty of "willful failure to file" charges by a jury in federal district court in Shreveport, La. July 11. The jury found Cryer not guilty of two counts of willful failure to file an income tax return for 2000 and 2001, which carried a two-year prison sentence.

Some 25 Cryer supporters from as far away as 1,200 miles came out to attend this critical trial, which tax honesty advocates are heralding as a big victory for the growing anti-IRS movement.

Day one commenced with Justice Department lawyers dropping two of the four charges filed against Cryer in the original indictment. This reduced the sentence he was facing from 10 years to two years in prison. In addition, there were fireworks that day during Cryer's testimony and the judge was clearly aggravated. Cryer and the judge argued about his right to present his beliefs to the jury. The judge warned Larry Becraft, Cryer's lawyer, about the "very narrow" path he's taking and would not allow Cryer to argue that the IRS is unconstitutional—which he never intended to do.

JUDGE VENTS ANGER

Day two ended with the judge calling Becraft into his chamber and venting his frustration for taking over the courtroom and plowing ahead with getting

nation of Cryer's beliefs.

Cryer explained to the jury that his study of the Constitution, Supreme Court decisions and IRS Code and regulations convinced him that he was not required to file or to pay the federal income tax, despite the fact that he made his living as an attorney.

The government lawyer never offered to refute the Supreme Court decisions or the IRS code and regulations that Cryer had relied on.

The Department of Justice walked out with years of Cryer's research that was condensed into a well-organized presentation, which showed that not only did Cryer believe his research, but confirmed the fact that there was no law making him liable for federal income taxes.

The jury believed Cryer was telling the truth and found him not guilty of the charges that the Justice Department had filed against him.

Cryer's case followed on the heels of another, which occurred approximately two years ago. A jury in a federal case in California dealt a blow to the IRS's image of invincibility by finding former IRS Criminal Investigator Joseph Banister not guilty of several tax charges. AFP reported in depth on that case in the July 11, 2005, issue.

★

Peymon Mottahedeh lives in California and is the founder and president of Freedom Law School. His ad for Freedom Law School runs every other week all year in the pages of American Free Press.

Rumor has it that so many Americans have delivered the following "Notice and Demand" to the IRS that it is fearful its own employees will lawfully stop volunteering to pay taxes on their income.

Fax this to the White House – 1-202-456-2461
Fax this to the Senate – 1-202-224-2262
Fax this to the House of Representatives – 1-202-225-0697

Tell them to tell the Internal Revenue Service – The IRS:

"IRS, the income tax is finished in America."

(Get the documented "Special Tax Issue" from Media Bypass – 1-812-477-8670)

(Or, fax this directly to the IRS Regional Offices yourself.):

Washington, DC	FAX 1-202-622-4355	Memphis, Tennessee	FAX 1-901-360-1828
Ogden, Utah	FAX 1-801-620-3096	Manassas, Virginia	FAX 1-703-368-9694
Patchogue, New York	FAX 1-631-654-6970	San Jose, California	FAX 1-408-817-6852
Denver, Colorado	FAX 1-303-446-1716	Los Angeles, California	FAX 1-213-576-3143

(Also IRS employees and others)

NOTICE AND OFFER

We Americans hereby notify you that we offer that you, the Internal Revenue Service, aka "IRS," complete amnesty if you permanently cease demanding a tax on our income, and close down your terrorist operations, for the following reasons:

- That you, IRS, have fraudulently, as a private Delaware corporation, along with the unratified Sixteenth Amendment to our Constitution, deceived the American people since 1913, saying that the "Income Tax" is mandatory, when, in fact, it is voluntary;
- That you, IRS, have sent terrorist agents throughout America to unlawfully and illegally harass and steal from her people by threats and extortion;
- That you, IRS, with your collections of so-called "income-tax money," which does not go to "run the government," have committed a terrible fraud against the American people. In fact, the so-called "tax monies" you have collected over the years have gone to the private Federal Reserve Banks (FED) and ended up in the pockets of the private international banking cartel;
- This, IRS, is totally and completely TREASON against our long-established traditions of liberty, which are anchored in the Constitution for the united States of America, with its permanent Bill of Rights.
- NOW THEREFORE, WE NOTIFY YOU THAT WE OFFER YOU COMPLETE AMNESTY IF YOU PERMANENTLY CLOSE DOWN TERRORIST OPERATIONS – AND NEVER AGAIN ATTEMPT TO EXTORT AN INCOME TAX FROM US.

The Governor of each State grants "AMNESTY".

> SENATOR HENRY BELLMON OF OK-
> LAHOMA—testifying before the Finance
> Committee October 2, 1969 said: "In a recent
> conversation with an official at the Internal
> Revenue Service. I was amazed when he told me
> that, 'If the taxpayers of this country ever
> discover that <u>the Internal Revenue Service
> operates on 90% bluff</u>, the entire system will
> collapse."

Taxes!   Taxes!   Taxes!
LET'S FIX IT!

Courageous former IRS Agent Joe Banister has broken the "Code of Silence" and has suffered for it. But it is all for nothing if you don't know what he wants to tell all free Americans.

When the IRS received Agent Banister's report, the IRS Washington, DC office demanded Joe Banister's immediate resignation.

For confirmation of IRS fraud/lies about the income tax, send a twenty dollar money order to former IRS enforcement agent Joe Banister and ask him for his 90-page report. (It took Joe two years to research this report.)

Joe Banister   C/0   <u>Media Bypass</u>
PO Box 5326
Evansville, IN 47716

108TH CONGRESS
1ST SESSION **H.J. RES. 15**

IN THE HOUSE OF REPRESENTATIVES
JANUARY 28, 2003

Mr. PAUL introduced the following joint resolution; which was
referred to the Committee on the Judiciary

JOINT RESOLUTION

Proposing <u>an amendment to the Constitution</u> of the United States relative to <u>abolishing personal income</u>, estate, and gift taxes and prohibiting the United States Government from engaging in business in competition with its citizens.

Resolved by the Senate and House of Representatives of the United States of America in Congress assembled (two-thirds of each House concurring therein), That the following article is proposed as an amendment to the Constitution of the United States, which shall be valid to all intents and purposes as part of the Constitution when ratified by the legislatures of three-fourths of the several States within seven years after the date of its submission for ratification:

ARTICLE —

"SECTION 1. The Government of the United States shall not engage in any business, professional, commercial, financial or industrial enterprise except as specified in the Constitution.

"SECTION 2. The constitution or laws of any State, or the laws of the United States, shall not be subject to the terms of any foreign or domestic agreement which would abrogate this amendment.

"SECTION 3. The activities of the United States Government which violate the intent and purposes of this amendment shall, within a period of three years from the date of the ratification of this amendment, be liquidated and the properties and facilities affected shall be sold.

"SECTION 4. Three years after the ratification of this amendment the sixteenth article of amendments to the Constitution of the United States shall stand repealed and thereafter Congress shall not levy taxes on personal incomes, estates, and/or gifts."

**Congress now has actual
notice of income tax evil
bob@givemeliberty.org**

On 15 April, 2002, citizens served all but 11 of the 535 Members of Congress with a copy of the record of the Citizens' *Truth – In – Taxation Hearing*. The packages contain the sworn video testimony and conclusive legal documentation that the IRS lacks the lawful authority to force employers to withhold the income tax from the paychecks' of their employees or to force Americans to file a tax return and to pay the tax. Each delivery was formally witnessed via an affidavit of process service.

Congress has now been officially put on notice by the People:

- The IRS lacks legal jurisdiction to enforce the federal income tax within the borders of the 50 states,
- The federal income tax system is unlawfully applied, and
- The IRS routinely violates peoples' Fourth Amendment due process rights.

Along with the record of the Hearing, the Congressmen received thousands of letters demanding they move, no later than June 1, 2002, to direct IRS and DOJ to either stop forcing employers to withhold and to stop forcing the People to file and pay, or schedule a full-blown congressional hearing requiring IRS and DOJ to appear and address the evidence from the Truth In Taxation Hearing record.

THE IRS lost a case
IRS vs. KUGLIN   Carl F. Worden

Forget the war in Iraq, Afghanistan and our excellent adventure in Liberia. The biggest news of the entire week is that on August 8, 2003, the IRS was unable to convince a jury in Memphis, Tennessee, that the Federal Tax Code requires the citizens to pay individual income taxes. I kid you not.

[Ed: Now read this paragraph again!]

I watched as many Sunday news programs as I could possibly stand, and I didn't hear a single mention of the IRS' debacle in Memphis. If you ever had doubts about the mainstream media being controlled by the federal government, doubt no more.

For those not already aware, FedEx Pilot Vernice Kuglin began studying the IRS Code some years ago, and was simply unable to find anywhere in the code that she was required to pay federal income taxes.

And here's the most remarkable part: Back in 1995, Kuglin wrote letters in good faith to the IRS, asking them to show her where the Tax Code requires individual citizens to pay federal income taxes. Incredibly the IRS never answered a single one of her letters!

As she studied the facts, laws and related documents more, Kuglin became convinced that, regardless of the IRS' failure to respond one way or the other, she was exempt from paying federal income taxes. So, Kuglin filled out W-4 forms showing 99 exemptions, and turned them in to her employer. Doing that meant Kuglin got to take home almost all of her paycheck each payday, instead of what was left after the feds ravaged it.

The IRS went after Kuglin for six counts of tax evasion on $920,000 income, and for filing "false" W-4 forms, charges that could have put the 58-year-old Kuglin in federal prison for up to 30 years and cost her 1.5 million in fines.

Apparently, things didn't go quite the slam-dunk way federal prosecutor Joe Murphy thought they would. My money says the IRS wishes they had never gone after Kuglin at all.

In fact, after the jury returned not guilty verdicts on all counts, Murphy is reported to have demanded that the judge order Kuglin to file her forms, pay her taxes and "obey the law". The judge reportedly replied, "Sir, I don't work for the IRS."

Now pinch yourself and review this astonishing turn of events.

A highly trained and educated federal prosecutor in Memphis was unable to convince 12 American citizens that Vernice Kuglin was required to pay federal income taxes. He was clearly unable to produce a single section of the Tax Code to that end, and the jury was unanimous in clearing Kuglin of all charges against her. If the foregoing was not so, Kuglin would have been convicted.

Jurors tend not to be very sympathetic with tax scofflaws, since each one of them is also a taxpayer and they understandably feel resentment towards anyone not paying "their fair share". So in order for this federal jury to completely vindicate Kuglin, the government's failure to prove their case against her had to have been clear and unequivocal!

I haven't read the trial transcript yet, but I must assume the federal prosecutor at least tried to twist some vague and ambiguous section of the Tax Code to make it look like it applied to Kuglin. I don't know that, but I'll bet he tried. What else could he use to prosecute her with?

[Ed: Maybe they tried with "Everybody knows they have to pay the income tax!"]

Thanks to the IRS' arrogance and stupidity, and Kuglin's refusal to plead to lesser charges, Kuglin accomplished what Bob Schultz and the other "tax protesters" had been denied all along: To force the IRS into a public debate and to answer the question of whether or not the Tax Code requires an individual to pay personal income taxes. Kuglin and her two attorneys, Larry Becraft and Robert Bernhoft, have unequivocally forced the IRS to show its hand, and 12 judges hearing that debate ruled the answer to be "NOT GUILTY"! on all 6 counts!

I think it's time for everyone reading this to send a very polite letter to the IRS, telling them they read about the case in Memphis, and is it true that there is no section in the U.S. Tax Code that requires an individual citizen to pay federal income taxes?

Don't be threatening in any way, or announce that you plan to stop paying federal income taxes. This request is for your personal edification, and you just simply want to know the truth.

Like Kuglin, you probably won't get an answer back, but just to prove you sent the letter and that they received it, be certain to send the letter via certified U.S. Mail, with a return receipt requested. When you get that receipt back, staple it to a copy of the letter you sent the IRS, and put it somewhere real secure, like a personal safe or bank deposit box. I don't have to explain why, now do I?

Spirit Lake, Idaho 83869
(208) 255-2307 FAX (208) 255-2607
E-Mail: observer@coldreams.com

Constitutional Crisis

"The people...are the only sure reliance for the preservation of our liberty."
Thomas Jefferson

Petition for redress of tax-related grievances ignored

Truth in Taxation Hearing held: IRS, DOJ refuse to participate

by Bob Schulz

WASHINGTON, D.C.—On February 27 and 28, 2002, at the Washington Marriott in Washington DC, the We The People Foundation for Constitutional Education sponsored the long-awaited Truth-in-Taxation Hearing. This historic event brought to public attention the facts about how the three branches of the federal government have intentionally and systematically conspired to deprive the American People of our Constitutional rights, and reduce our citizens to indentured servants of a corrupt federal government bureaucracy.

The hearing was but another step in the People's determination to get to the truth regarding the fraudulent origin and operation of the Federal Reserve System, the unconstitutional creation of the Internal Revenue Service, and the illegal operations of our nation's income tax system.

Expert witnesses testified, under oath, to various questions challenging the legal authority of the IRS to force employers to withhold any income tax from the paychecks of their employees and the legal authority of the IRS to force most American citizens to file a tax return and to pay the income tax.

The Foundation's objective was to establish a factual record, to be used by the People in support of their future actions regarding the income tax.

Although we had hoped to have hostile witnesses from DOJ and IRS answer our questions as they agreed to in July, 2001, they arrogantly refused to appear before We The People in this recorded, public forum to answer our questions.

From the Record of the hearing, the reason is obvious; DOJ and IRS could

and ultimately repugnant to every principle of equal justice, due process of law and personal liberty that we cherish as Americans.

The proof was, as predicted: startling, compelling, disturbing and irrefutable.

The record of the hearing proves conclusively for history:

"The Internal Revenue Code does not make most Americans liable to file a tax return and pay an income tax.

"People have a right to the fruits of their labor; the income tax is a slave tax, and is prohibited by the 13th Amendment.

"Congress lacks the authority to legislate an income tax on the people except in the District of Columbia, the U.S. Territories and in those geographic areas within any of the 50 states where the States have specifically approved it, in writing. No legislative jurisdiction means no taxing authority.

"There is no income tax exception to the 5th Amendment's guarantee of the Peoples' unalienable right not to be compelled to be a witness against themselves; individuals do, in fact, waive their 5th Amendment (Miranda) right not to be a witness against themselves when they sign and file a Form 1040 tax return.

Personal income taxes polarize and divide an otherwise united nation and promote class warfare and 'mistrust of our government.

"The IRS, the courts and even the NY Times cite the 16th Amendment as government's authority to impose a tax directly on the People's labor. However, the 16th Amendment did not come close to being lawfully ratified by ¾ of the states as constitutionally required, and was fraudulently declared to have been ratified in 1913 by Philander Knox, the Secretary of State. The 16th Amendment is null and void.

We demonstrated the power of the People to use mass media to effectively counter government propaganda.

We even demonstrated the power of the People to trump the power of the traditional T.V. - the medium of choice by the government and those who prefer to quote officialdom, (rather than the People); NBC, ABC, CBS, PBS and the major cable companies.

The Technology

In addition to the historical content of the hearing, cutting-edge multi-media and internet technologies were integrated and deployed in a unique combination for the first time to virtually eliminate the need to attend the hearings in person.

Viewers on the internet could not only see and hear the proceedings live via a professionally produced video broadcast, but could simultaneously see the text of the questions being asked and access live "hyperlinks" to the actual evidence as it was presented at the hearing.

In this way, viewers at home or the office across America could independently download, view and/or print usable copies of the evidence, independent of the video streaming. In fact, the webcast software and evidence database were used live in the hearing room to project the evidence to the audience and those testifying on a series of projection screens and monitors.

Remote access to individual webcast streams was controlled via passwords and user-ids that were generated electronically at the time of purchase. Purchases were made via a secure, customized on-line e-commerce system.

The Foundation believes its successful demonstration of these technologies may mark a significant leap in the ability of the freedom movement to organize, communicate and broadcast all while bypassing

We The People are entitled to a system of taxation that is constitutional in its construction, lawful in its administration, and just in its effect. We are a sovereign people with deep respect for our unalienable right to life, liberty and property through responsible citizenship. We The People reject the proposition that government is entitled to control any part of our lives or property without our consent. We do not recognize a majority vote as a license for government to abuse its limited constitutional authority. Under our constitutional form of government, we acknowledge and honor the proposition that all men are created equal, and that every American citizen is endowed with certain unalienable rights that cannot be lawfully denied by majority vote. But we can only hope to achieve honest, accountable government, and a lawful system of taxation in our nation if we build a critical mass of knowledge and awareness among our people.

We The People Foundation For Constitutional Education, Inc. fought with fierce determination to give the American People the truth-in-taxation hearing on February 27-28 in Washington, DC. Against overwhelming odds, and at tremendous financial costs, we have completely exposed how the Department of Justice, the Internal Revenue Service, Congress, the Federal Courts, and the politically controlled major media, all turned their backs on our Constitution and the American People. The hearing was a great success for our nation and the cause of freedom. We will now move forward to build the critical mass of awareness required to destroy this fraudulent income tax system, and the culture of government abuse and criminal conduct that it has produced in our society.

Please understand that the Foundation

not answer the questions truthfully without admitting to the fraudulent jurisdiction of the IRS and the illegal operation of the income tax system.

Instead, we asked independent expert witnesses to answer the questions that the Department of Justice, Internal Revenue Service, Congress and the Federal Courts have steadfastly refused to confront publicly.

The witnesses at the hearing were highly credible, educated experts who have extensive legal and technical expertise and first hand knowledge of the abuses the American people are suffering under our unlawful and abusive income tax system.

The expert witnesses included constitutional and tax attorneys (Larry Becraft, Paul Chappell and Noel Spaid), Certified Public Accountants (Joseph Banister, Victoria Osborn and Sherry Jackson), former IRS agents (Joseph Banister, Sherry Jackson and John Turner) and tax law researchers and authors (Bill Benson and Irwin Schiff).

As thousands of citizens across the country watched the live web broadcast of this historic truth-in-taxation hearing, the irrefutable truth about the fraudulent origin and unlawful operation and enforcement of the income tax system unfolded with every piece of compelling documentary evidence and sworn expert testimony.

The factual record established at the hearing is absolutely conclusive and irrefutable. From the professional credentials and sworn testimony of the expert witnesses, the exhaustive citations of constitutional and case law, the comprehensive review of statutory definitions, the extensive list of certified government documents, the presentation of over 500 legal questions—each in the form of a statement of legal fact, the truth-in-taxation hearing proved conclusively that the federal government has perpetrated a massive fraud against the American People.

The hearing record should now remove any doubt by anyone (including Congress, the Department of Justice and the Federal Courts) that the nation's income tax system is unconstitutional in its origin, fraudulent and abusive in its operation,

"The IRS routinely violates the 4th Amendment due process and privacy protections of Americans by seizing assets without lawful authority or a court order and by denying citizens their right to statutorily-prescribed, administrative remedies.

"The IRS willfully and intentionally manipulates taxpayers' Individual Master Files for the purpose of creating time-barred assessments, creating and providing fraudulent certificates of official records to the court to support illegal assessments, manipulating master files to short-pay taxpayers' legal interest owed by the government, collecting social security from taxpayers via levy in direct violation of the law, willful and intentional creation of fraudulent penalty and interest against taxpayers, and willful and intentional violation of taxpayers rights to due process.

"The IRS, without legal authority, routinely and illegally prepares "dummy returns" with inflated assessments for taxpayers who legitimately do not file a tax return as a means of punishing those who stand on their legal rights in choosing not to file.

The leverage of this historic hearing will go far beyond the record it created and become the central focus of the Peoples' next steps to end the illegal income tax system. Details of specific legal actions being taken in response to both the hearing findings and the government's refusal to respond to the Petition for Redress of Grievances will be released during the next week.

The power of the hearing was also a demonstration of the physical might of the communications channel used to broadcast the hearing - the world-wide-web and the personal computer. Thousands of people across this nation witnessed this hearing live.

We demonstrated that the People are no longer dependent upon the dominant broadcast media, including C-SPAN, to transmit to thousands of widely separated electronic receivers, at the same time, transient images of moving objects together with sound, on a 24 hour, seven day per week basis if necessary.

the established media providers such as C-SPAN, network news, etc. The ability to transmit, both live and delayed, coverage of key freedom events should prove extremely beneficial in our collective fight to elevate the Constitution to its rightful place in our society, and to strengthen our Republic through education.

Many thanks go to Scott Hildebrandt of e-knowledge, Inc. for developing the webcast and webcast management systems.

Obtain Copies of the Record.

For a minimal donation to the Foundation, copies of the full hearing/record can be obtained now on CD-ROM and VHS tape. See ad below to obtain copies of the record.

The CD-ROM versions will contain copies of all the evidence as well as a large volume of supporting materials that most will find very valuable. Obviously, the VHS tapes cannot include copies of the evidence and can only include a video/audio record of the sworn testimony and questioning in the hearing room.

We encourage people to request multiple copies of the CD-ROMs and/or the tapes and to share them with people they know and to request of those people that they do the same.

has incurred substantial expenses over the past 7 months in bringing these truths to the American People. We have incurred hundreds of thousands of dollars in direct expenses related the webcast technology, the hearing facilities, travel expenses, attorneys, advertising, and so forth. Countless people selflessly volunteered their time and resources to make the truth-in-taxation hearing a reality. As you know, We The People Foundation is an educational organization and does not sell products or services for a profit. We have no paid staff and must rely on the support of volunteers and donations from those who share our love of Country, commitment to our constitution, and dedication to the cause of freedom. Every dollar we receive in donations goes directly to pay hard expenses in our vigilant fight to protect and defend those principles of equality, justice and liberty for which we, as Americans, stand. We must now ask for your financial help. We need your direct financial donations and your purchase of copies of the recording of the hearing. Please help us at this critical hour in the life of our nation. We must stand together and use our collective resources if we are to prevail in this eternal fight for liberty.

Idaho Observer | PO Box 457
Spirit Lake, Idaho 83869
(208) 255-2307 FAX (208) 255-2607
E-Mail: observer@coldreams.com

The IRS assault on churches and Christians in America

The Rev, Texe Marrs is a Christian activist and hea LIVING TRUTH MINISTRIES at 1708 Patterson Austin, Texas 78733. He publishes a news le FLASHPOINT, and writes and sells religious mate and books.

In the current issue of FREE AMERIC MAGAZINE, U.S. Hwy. 380, Box 2943 Bingl New Mexico, 87832, Mr. Marrs recounts the investigation his organization is experiencing – an things the IRS says he CANNOT do and contint operate as a tax exempt Church and ministry:

1. Expose conspiracies.
2. Criticize the New World Order.
3. Say anything negative about a politician, Republican or Democrat.
4. Criticize any government agency.
5. Criticize any institution of government, including White House and Supreme Court
6. Encourage citizens to call or write their congressmen, mayor, governor, etc.
7. Criticize any proposed bill or legislation tha would take away people's rights.
8. Criticize the New Age Movement.
9. Support or encourage law-abiding citizen's militias.
10. Make any critical remarks about any other religious movement or faith.
11. Support or encourage the right of the peopl bear arms; the Second Amendment.
12. Discourage girls from getting an abortion o support the pro-life movement.
13. Teach abortion is murder, especially partial birth abortions.
14. Identify homosexuality as a sin.
15. Express an opinion on any political subject issue.
16. Preach "fire & brimstone", or other evange sermons, unless considered a "reasoned approach" by the IRS.
17. Identify threats to Christianity, or discuss th
18. Discuss subjects the IRS terms "sensational
19. Criticize public figures and institutions the deems "worthy".
20. Publish or broadcast on any topic without giving equal time to opposing views.

21. Publish and offer books, tapes or products that expose an elitist plot against humanity or God.
22. Criticize the Pope or the Vatican, or contrast the New Catholic Catechism to beliefs found in the Holy Bible.
23. Criticize the United Nations or such global groups as The council on Foreign Relations, the Bilderbergers or the Trilateral Commission.
24. Criticize the Masonic Lodge, Skull & Bones or any other secret society.
25. Bring to public attention immorality in government or other public officials.
26. Complain of government wrong-doing or injustice, such as Waco and Ruby Ridge.
27. Criticize the Zionist ADL and any other Zionist group.
28. Say anything positive about the "religious right" or "patriot movement".
29. Support home schooling, unregistered churches and home churches.
30. Spend money on missionary work or public charities not approved by the IRS.
31. Promote or encourage alternative medicines or health care (herbs, etc.).
32. Expose false teachings on anything by anyone.
33. Support or expose Christian persecution and suffering under anti-Christian governments.
34. Advocate or support any Bible doctrine that is politically or religiously incorrect, or inconsistent with public policy currently being "enforce" by the IRS.
35. Ordain a pastor whose training and qualifications are not approved by the IRS.

I know Clayton Douglas, publisher of the FREE AMERICAN. He takes his responsibilities to his readers very seriously, and he would not publish the above list without verifying it as fact.

I also receive Texe Marrs FLASHPOINT, and am quite familiar with his views – and I am not alarmed by what he says or writes.

The point is, whether one agrees with either, neither or both, the actions of the IRS are very alarming. Certainly more of a threat to our liberty that Texe or Clayton.

Now there are five renegade IRS agents

It must have been very, very hard for these successful tax-collectors to come to the conclusion that what they were doing was wrong.

Oh, it's not wrong to collect taxes. They know this. But these tax collectors found that there is no law that says you owe a cut of your wages as "income" tax.

All five of them had to check this out for themselves. The Internal Revenue Service did not tell it to them, of course.

Joseph R. Banister

Clifton Beale

Paul Chappell

Sherry P. Jackson

John Turner

Honor these fine renegades as brave pioneers of liberty. There will be more.

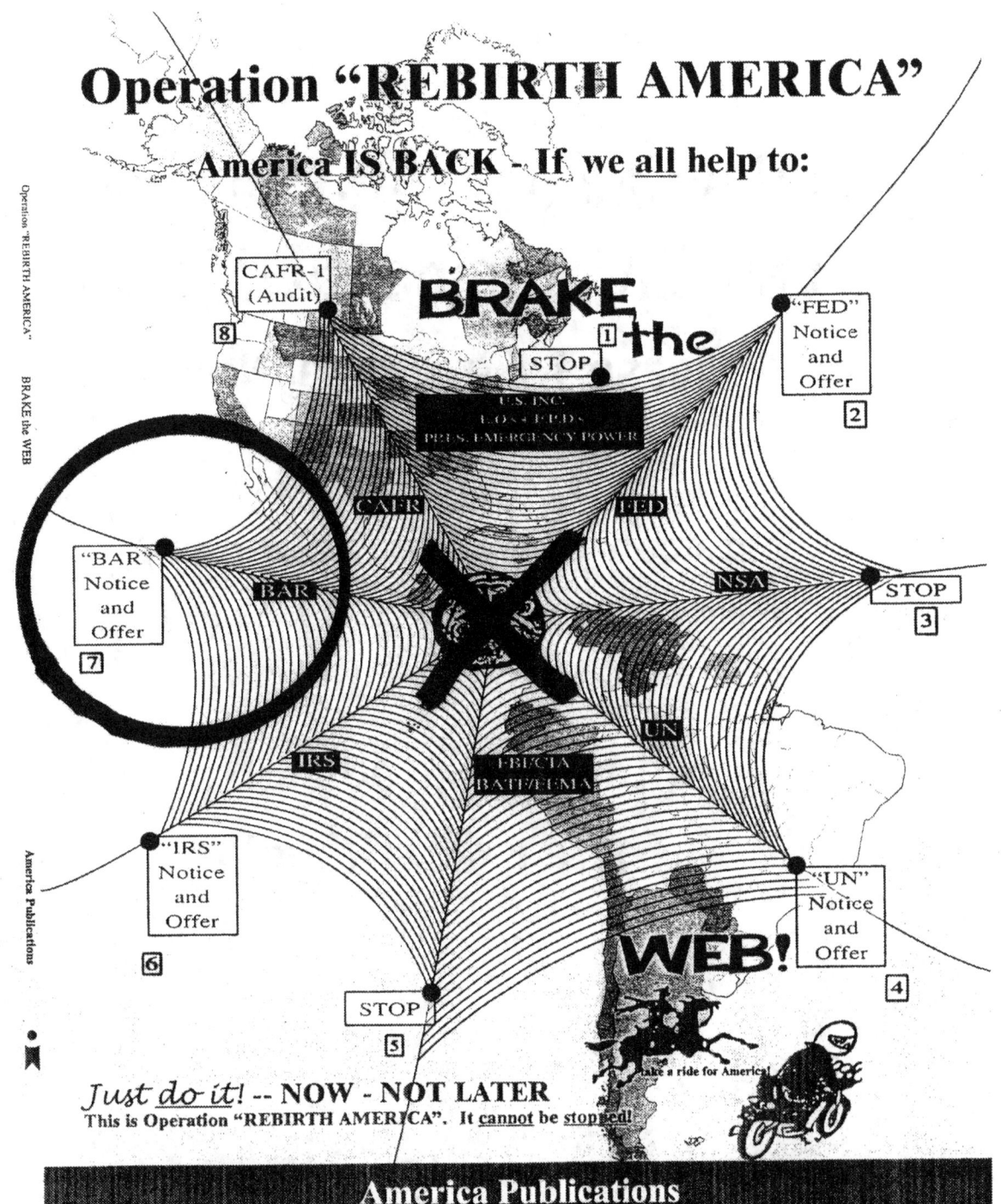

Operation "REBIRTH AMERICA"

America IS BACK - If we all help to:

BRAKE the WEB!

- CAFR-1 (Audit) [8]
- "FED" Notice and Offer [2]
- STOP [1]
- STOP [3]
- "BAR" Notice and Offer [7]
- "IRS" Notice and Offer [6]
- STOP [5]
- "UN" Notice and Offer [4]

US INC. LOST FEDS PRES. EMERGENCY POWER

CAFR FED NSA UN BAR IRS FBI/CIA BATF/FEMA

Just do it! -- **NOW - NOT LATER**
This is Operation "REBIRTH AMERICA". It cannot be stopped!

Juries, Judges, Attorneys and Law Enforcement Officers

- Please Take Special Note -

When there is a case
between **Liberty** and slavery,
the decision MUST ALWAYS
be in favor of **Liberty**!

With NO Injured Party, There Is NO Crime!

Fax this to the White House – 1-202-456-2461
Fax this to the Senate – 1-202-224-2262
Fax this to the House of Representatives – 1-202-225-0697

Fax this to tell them to tell the State, Federal and International "Bar" Associations

"BAR, your monopoly control over attorneys and judges is finished in America. Drop it!"

(Or, fax this yourself and tell the "Bar" and its controlled Schools of Law.)

-- Bar Associations and Law Schools --
(Also, for all law school students, BAR employees and others.)
(Or, fax this to your "favorite" federal or State court.)

NOTICE AND OFFER

We Americans hereby <u>notify</u> you, "The Bar", aka State Bar Associations, Federal Bar Association and International Bar Association, with your judge, attorney and Law School members, that we <u>offer</u> you complete amnesty if you immediately close down your illegal and unlawful monopoly associations in America for the following reasons:

- That you, BAR, are secretly controlled from England, all the way down to the newest attorney just out of Law School;
- That you, BAR, have gone against the Constitution of these united States by promoting "titles of nobility" (i.e., "esquire") and pretending to make attorneys actual positions in our federal, State and local governments;
- That you, BAR, with your attorney and judge members, have illegally and unlawfully subverted and manipulated court cases and legislation in direct violation of State and federal Constitutional law;
- That you, BAR, have wrongfully influenced the removal from our Law Schools, the teachings of our Constitution and its <u>permanent</u> Bill of Rights;
- That you, BAR, have illegally and unlawfully fed your member attorneys and judges the false doctrine of immunity from accountability for their actions, both in and out of the courtrooms of America.

NOW THEREFORE, WE <u>NOTIFY</u> YOU THAT WE <u>OFFER</u> YOU COMPLETE AMNESTY IF   YOU CLOSE DOWN YOUR UNLAWFUL AND ILLEGAL MONOPOLY OPERATIONS IN AMERICA, IMMEDIATELY.

The Governor of each State grants "AMNESTY".

"Remember, where you have a concentration of
power in a few hands, all too frequently men
with the mentality of gangsters get control.
History has proven that. All power corrupts;
absolute power corrupts absolutely."
—*Lord Acton* (1870)

British Accredited Registry (BAR)?

During the middle 1600's, the Crown of England established a formal registry in London where barristers were ordered by the Crown to be accredited. The establishment of this first International Bar Association allowed barrister-lawyers from all nations to be formally recognized and accredited by the only recognized accreditation society. From this, the acronym BAR was established denoting (informally) the British Accredited Registry, whose members became a powerful and integral force within the International Bar Association (IBA). Although this has been denied repeatedly as to its existence, the acronym BAR stood for the British barrister-lawyers who were members of the larger IBA

When America was still a chartered group of British colonies under patent – established in what was formally named the British Crown territory of New England – the first British Accredited Registry (BAR) was established in Boston during 1761 to attempt to allow only accredited barrister-lawyers access to the British courts of New England. This was the first attempt to control who could represent defendants in the court at or within the bar in America.

Today, each corporate STATE in America has it's own BAR Association, *i.e.* The Florida Bar or the California Bar, that licenses government officer attorneys, NOT lawyers. In reality, the U.S. courts only allow their officer attorneys to freely enter *within* the bar while prohibiting those learned of the law – lawyers – to do so. They prevent advocates, lawyers, counselors, barrister and solicitors from entering through the outer bar. *Only* licensed BAR Attorneys are permitted to freely enter within the bar separating the people from the bench because all BAR Attorneys are officers of the court itself. Does that tell you anything?

Here's where the whole word game gets really tricky. In each State, every licensed BAR Attorney calls himself an Attorney at Law. Look at the definitions above and see for yourself that an Attorney at Law is nothing more than an attorney – one who transfers allegiance and property to the ruling land owner.

Another name game they use is "of counsel," which means absolutely nothing more than an offer of advice. Surely, the mechanic down the street can do that! Advice is one thing; lawful representation is another.

A BAR licensed Attorney is *not* an advocate, so how can he do anything other than what his real purpose is? He can't plead on your behalf because there would be a conflict of interest. He can't represent the crown (ruling government) as an official officer at the same time he is allegedly representing a defendant. His sworn duty as a BAR Attorney is to transfer your ownership, rights, titles, and allegiance to the land owner. When you hire a BAR Attorney to represent you in their courts, you have hired an officer of that court whose sole purpose and occupation is to transfer what you have to the creator and authority of that court. A more appropriate phrase would be legal plunder.

"Government is not reason; it is not eloquence;
it is force! Like fire, it is a dangerous
servant and a fearful master."
— *George Washington*

Will Florida be the first state to disembowel the Bar?

Persistent grassroots activist may have started movement to end legal monopoly

MIAMI LAKE, Fla.—By persistently distributing his bumper stickers and pamphleteering in courthouses all over Florida, Robert Bertrand of the National Congress for Legal Reform has created a critical mass of public opinion that could result in the state decommissioning its Bar association. "We have started a movement that is spreading all over the country," said Bertrand.

Bertrand, 61, who started his crusade in 1986 when friends committed suicide after lawyers took everything in their divorces, has perfected the manner in which the public can be educated about how lawyers have taken over all three branches of government. He suggests that people read the *Federalist Papers*, the *Anti-Federalist Papers* and the material on his websites. "Then go down and get a rubber stamp that says, 'Help Save America. Don't Vote for Lawyers' and stamp everything you send out in the mail," Bertrand advised.

Our nation, Bertrand explained, is suffering from an epidemic of "cognitive dissonance." Most people don't like lawyers, don't trust lawyers and tell lawyers jokes every chance they get—but then they go down and vote them into public office.

James Madison, one of the authors of the *Federalist Papers*, was charged with the task of creating a government with enough power to control, but not enough power to oppress. He stressed the importance of the separation of powers. He knew that a government where the same hands are allowed to make, interpret and enforce the laws is a government that will oppress its people. "The enemy is us, we have allowed lawyers to take over control of all three branches of government," said Bertrand.

Bertrand is considering the possibility of promoting a bill that would make reading the *Federalist Papers* and the *Anti-Federalist Papers* a requirement of graduation from public school. "Once students read the *Federalist Papers*, 95 percent of them agree that lawyers should not be allowed to occupy positions in the legislative or executive branches of government (the other five percent are the sons and daughters of attorneys).

Tele. (305) 534-1362;   *The James Madison Foundation,* 3720 Collins Ave., Miami Bch., FL 33140; www. calhounreport.com/ email: novoteatty@mindspring.com/

The Idaho Observer

PO Box 457
Spirit Lake, Idaho 83869
(208) 255-2307 FAX (208) 255-2607
E-Mail: observer@cdreams.com

Hear Ye! Hear Ye! Rally Scheduled

A rally will be held at the Supreme Court on May 6, 2001 at 2:00 p.m. by an organization called A Matter of Justice, Inc., a national legal reform organization whose website is at www.amatterofjustice.org.

The protest will be against judicial immunity, the dysfunctional system of justice in this country and the corruption within the legal profession. Any questions call Dr. Jacob Roginsky at 540-644-9054 or David Grossack at 781-925-5253.

MJB Staff Report

A Matter of Justice /
Phone + FAX: (540) 644-9054
web site: www.amatterofjustice.org,
Box 6963 / Washington, D.C. 20077-9330.

J.A.I.L. for Judges

J.A.I.L. is an acronym for (Judicial Accountability Initiative Law)
JAIL's very informative website is found at www.jail4judges.org
JAIL proposes a unique new addition to our form of government.
JAIL is powerful! JAIL is dynamic! JAIL is America's ONLY hope!
JAIL is spreading across America like a fast moving wildfire!
JAIL is making inroads into Congress for federal accountability!
JAIL may be supported at P.O. Box 207, N. Hollywood, CA 91603

To send published judicial articles:
   USA-jail4judges@mindspring.com
To contact the author of JAIL4Judges:
   jail4judges@mindspring.com
All E-Groups are encouraged to sign on at
jail4judges@egroups.com

Those in power view ordinary people as resources, like fish or row crops; laws and taxes are simply how they harvest us.
—(DWH)

63

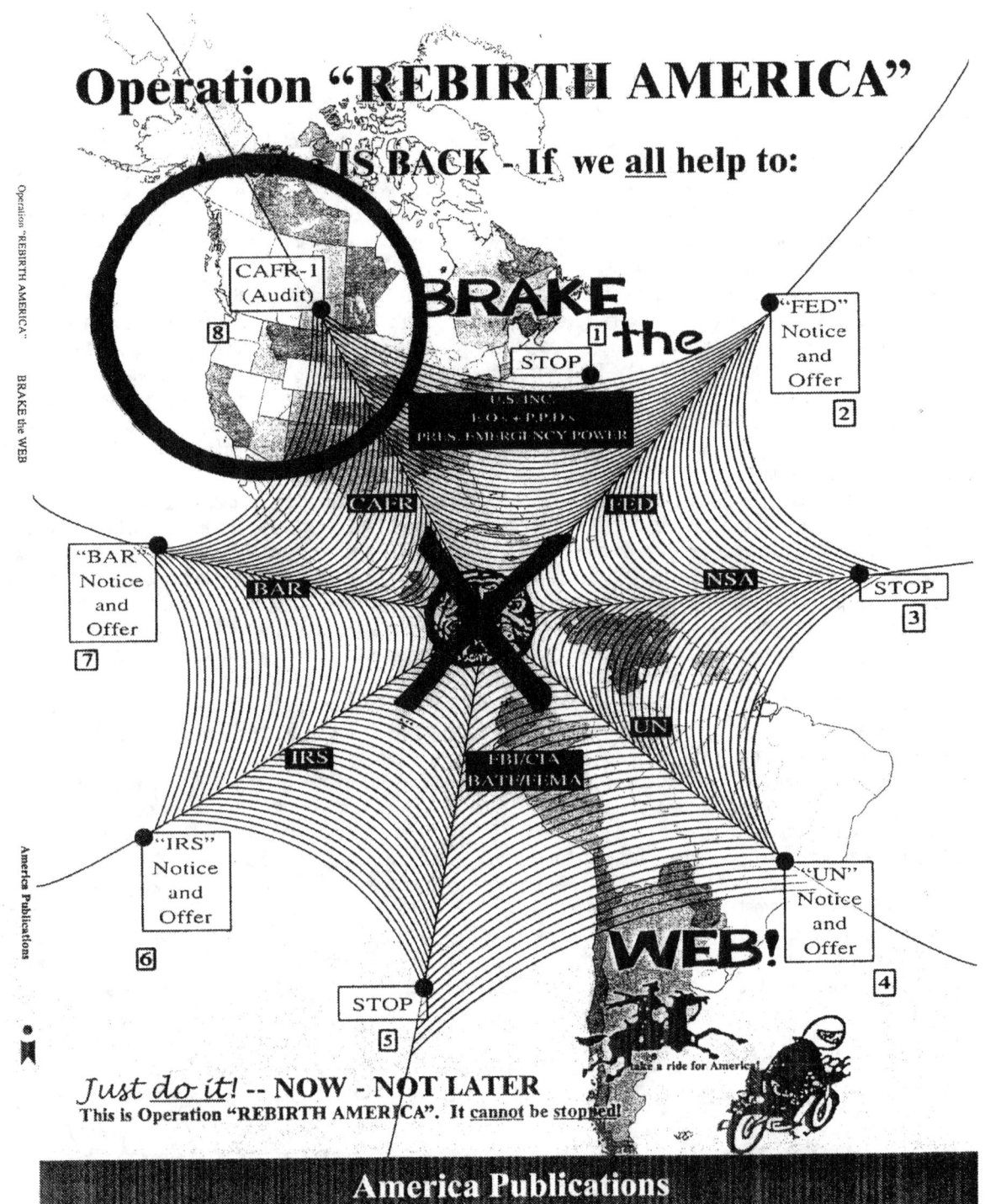

Operation "REBIRTH AMERICA"

IS BACK - If we all help to:

BRAKE the WEB!

CAFR-1 (Audit) 8

"FED" Notice and Offer 2

STOP 1

U.S. INC.
E.O.s + P.P.Ds
PRES. EMERGENCY POWER

CAFR FED

"BAR" Notice and Offer 7

BAR NSA STOP 3

IRS FBI/CIA BATF/FEMA UN

"IRS" Notice and Offer 6

"UN" Notice and Offer 4

STOP 5

Just do it! -- NOW - NOT LATER
This is Operation "REBIRTH AMERICA". It cannot be stopped!

Take a ride for America!

ASSAULT ON AMERICAN CHILDREN

On an infant's day of birth, it receives 12 mcgs of Mercury in the Hepatitis B shot. This is 30 times what the EPA defines as a "safe" level. American children have received 237 micrograms of mercury through vaccinations by age two, 30 vaccines by 18 months and 72 vaccines by age 6. Toxins are being injected directly into the bloodstream of infants and children whose brain, nervous system, immune system, reproductive and detoxification system (among others) are still developing, and who do not have a fully-functioning blood-brain barrier. The health consequences of this have never been researched or studied in any controlled or systematic way.

Adjuvants are toxic substances added to a vaccine or drug formulation which affects the action of the active ingredient in a predictable way. Some of these typical adjuvants routine in vaccinations are known neurotoxins and hormone disruptors. They include: Phenol, Formaldehyde, Alum, Acetone, Aluminum, Glycerin, MSG, Cadmium, Mercury (as thimerosal- the 3rd most deadly toxin and banned by the FDA in over-the-counter-drugs in 1998), Fecal matter, Horse serum, Calf serum, Dog kidney, Rabbit brain, and many more. Growth mediums include: Virus gathered from sick persons or animal from urine, blood, puss or feces which must be grown on a decomposing medium. Used for this purpose are aborted baby lung tissue, monkey kidneys and chick embryos. It is then preserved with toxins that are unnatural, immune suppressing and many times carcinogenic.

Why do millions of parents go along with this murder by injection? The answer is: The medical system intimidates parents by telling them that vaccinations are mandatory. The American people are out of the alternative health loop. Less than 2% have the facts about the danger. They do not read private research (alternative Health Newsletters) thus only know what the controlled media wants them to know. Parents believe that their children will not be allowed in schools (public or private) without the prescribed vaccinations. Vaccinations are long-term injuries. Later in life, serious illness and degenerative diseases appear (ah, this is the pharmaceuticals' grand design - automatic repeat business).

Vaccinations and the health consequences are in most cases separated by time. This confuses cause and effect. That is, the vaccination is never related to illness a few months to many years later - *the Perfect Crime*. We see babies being born pre-disposed to neurological problems. More children suffer from asthma, learning problems hyper activity, juvenile diabetes,. Autism, etc. Children have never been so chronically ill. What's more, even when death or injury occurs following a vaccination (as is often the case), the official line is always that no causative relationship can be proved.

Why do big pharmaceuticals engage in this crippling and murder by injection? It's greed! It's a $3 billion + annual industry. And it supports the medical system which the drug companies own. Why does the federal government support universal vaccinations, even paying each state a bonus of $100 for every fully vaccinated child? In a fascist state such as modern America, there is a marriage between big government and big industry. The propaganda of the corporate state manipulates the public mind to believe that ·public policy" is good for them when in fact the people are always manipulated against their best interest.

Let's come to our senses. These medical satanists are illegally assaulting our children and even infants. Refuse to sign the papers they push at you. They won't dare to vaccinate if you don't take the risk. Above all, don't vaccinate your new baby in the hospital. The blood brain barrier is very undeveloped and provides no protection against these toxins.

For a 120 minute video *"Vaccines: What CDC Documents and Science Reveal."* and/or the cassette tape *"The Dangers of Vaccines and How You Can Legally Avoid Them."* by Dr. Sherri Tenpenny call 440-239-1878 or visit www.nmaseminars.com. At the end of the video you'll find excellent information on how to access the vaccination laws for every state.

The above are excerpts from a recent *BOB LIVINGSTON LETTER*, which provides timely information on a variety of subjects.

The letter is published monthly at $39 per year. Sample issues are $6. Contact:

THE BOB LIVINGSTON LETTER, P.O. Box 110013, Birmingham, AL 35211

By Walter J. Burien Jr.

Government CAUGHT With "Second Set Of Books" Called "CAFR"

The Biggest Game in Town

The $60 Trillion CAFR "Investment" Breakdown:

Comprehensive Annual Financial Reports Exposed

Are you aware that 30 years ago only 8 to 12 percent of the financial activity and ownership of our nation resulted from the activity of the government, but today the figure is conservatively 48 percent?

We the People have been victimized by the largest organized syndicate on the face of the Earth.

CAFR – 1 (Audit)

The CAFR1 plan begins with a team of assigned independent auditors utilizing the standing laws for access to required financial disclosure. They will make a complete and thorough review of the current and past records held by the selected county and local governments within the jurisdiction of their county. This audit will not require approval or permission from a city council or the county board of supervisors. An independent team of auditors will not ask permission of the foxes to audit the hen house and then debate how many chickens are being eaten by the foxes. The hen house is audited Period!

With the raw data now in hand, the CAFR1 team will go to an Institutional Investment Banking group, or Insurance Conglomerate to have them verify the data collected, and within the second review, identify additional revenue or equity assets that were missed.

The first county selected for application of the plan presented through the prospectus will make that county a self-sufficient government inclusive with all cities, school districts and authorities within the jurisdiction of that county, done by the voter's approval for ratification by constitutional amendment.

The annuity fund will have an initial starting balance from the surplus revenues identified. Revenue raised from the sale of enterprise or venture projects held by government should be in the hands of the private sector, and revenue made available where downsizing is called for and appropriate. It will be emphasized up front that when the CAFR1 plan goes out for voter approval, due to the importance of the vote, all voters are to sign and date their voting card for the purpose of eliminating any chances of voter fraud or vote tampering.

As Mr. Burien noted in his presentation, composite government pension funds from the over 85,000 separate government operations, generated in 1999 a return substantially greater than all personal and corporate taxation collected from both local and federal government.

"They have accomplished already the structure and ability to implement the CAFR1 plan," Burien said. "With administrative action applied, government becomes self-sufficient, the public receives 100 percent productivity value for their labors, and the pool of investment wealth is now additionally enhanced to create the most stable, prosperous economy that could be possibly imagined."

Once the model is approved, and under operation on the playing field, the blueprinted model, _written in stone_ for its fundamental and basic application which makes the selected local government self sufficient without taxation, and creates the potential for a dividend return on top of no taxation, can then be distributed across the country for further and direct application elsewhere.

When completed in one county, that blueprint can be distributed across the country to become the standard, for every city, county and state. With one model in place, up and running, it can happen across the country overnight by true force of public will and mandate. Additionally, by performance comparison, local government operations will have to maintain high standards by comparison with other cities, counties and states successes in the elimination of taxation and return on investment.

When the aspect of the annuity pension fund goes into play to phase out and then eliminate taxation, an association will be made available to all residents from any city, county or state. An association composed of several large investment, banking and insurance firms to review any city, county or state for draft prospectus creation, and expedient implementation of the CAFR1 plan.

Mr. Burien used an excellent example during his presentation where he laid out on a table his pocket change entitling it the "Rainy Day Fund," and then next to and separate from the pocket change he put a stack of hundred dollar bills. He continued to direct the listeners' attention to the Rainy Day Fund quoting the typical government jargon as to this specific item until someone from the crowd asked insistently, "What is the stack of $100 dollar bills?"

Mr. Burien then laid out groups of the $100s identifying capital group areas never mentioned or talked about to the public, but kept in all effects exclusively secret between the inside players and controllers of that revenue, revenue which made the Rainy Day Fund truly pocket change in comparison.

For more information, contact Walter Burien by e-mail at CAFR1@aol.com. He can also be contacted by writing to PO Box 11444 Prescott, Arizona 86304. Visit the CAFR1 home page at http://members.aol.com/_ht_a/cafr1/CAFR.html.

The Web of Treason

The following pages represent other strands in the "Web of Treason" against America and other sovereign Nations and States.

When the light of truth and the light of understanding are known by all people, worldwide, then the "EXIT PLAN" toward the "REBIRTH" of liberty and justice, FOR ALL, will begin.

It is estimated this "REBIRTH EXIT PLAN" of repair may take up to 40 years to complete.

Remember: God plus one = a majority!

out of the war, must be used as a means to control the volume of money. To accomplish this, the bonds must be used as a banking basis. We are now awaiting for the Secretary of the Treasury to make his recommendation to Congress. It will not do to allow the greenback, as it is called, to circulate as money any length of time, as we cannot control that."

1863: President Abraham Lincoln discovers the Tsar of Russia, Alexander II (1855-1881), has been having problems with the Rothschilds as well, as he had been refusing their continual attempts to set up a central bank in Russia. The Tsar then gives President Lincoln some unexpected help.

The Tsar issues orders that if either England or France actively intervene in the American Civil War, and help the South, Russia would consider such action a declaration of war, and take the side of President Lincoln. To show that he wasn't messing about, he sends part of his Pacific Fleet to port in San Francisco and another part to port in New York.

The Rothschild banking house in Naples, Italy, C. M. de Rothschild e figli, closes following the unification of Italy.

The Rothschilds use one of their own in America, John D. Rockefeller, to form an oil business called Standard Oil which eventually takes over all of its competition.

1864: President Lincoln is re-elected on November 8th and on November 21st he writes a friend the following,

"The money power preys upon the nations in times of peace and conspires against it in times of adversity. It is more despotic than monarchy, more insolent than autocracy, more selfish than bureaucracy."

Rothschild agent, August Belmont, who by now is the Democratic Party's National Chairman (1860-1872), supports General George McClellan as the Democratic nominee to run against President Abraham Lincoln in this year's election. Much to the anger of Belmont, President Lincoln wins the election.

1865: In a statement to Congress, President Abraham Lincoln states,

"I have two great enemies, the Southern Army in front of me, and the financial institutions in the rear. Of the two, the one in my rear is my greatest foe."

On April 14th, forty-one days after his second inauguration, and just five days after General Lee surrendered to General Grant at Appomattox, President Lincoln is shot by John Wilkes Booth, at Ford's Theater. He would later die of his injuries, less than two months before the end of the American Civil War.

More than seventy years later, Booth's granddaughter

2001: On January 20th, only hours before leaving office, President Clinton grants Marc Rich (a Crypto-Zionist from Belgium, real name Marc Reich) an extremely controversial presidential pardon. In 1983, Marc Reich was indicted by United States Attorney and future mayor of New York City, Rudolph Giuliani, on charges of tax evasion and illegal trading with Iran. He fled to Switzerland before a court appearance, and remained on the FBI's "Most Wanted List" for many years.

Anti-Defamation League (ADL) National Director Abraham Foxman admits that his organization had received $250,000 in contributions from Marc Rich during a sixteen year period, including a grant of $100,000 shortly after Foxman had agreed to assist Rich in obtaining a presidential pardon from Bill Clinton. Foxman also admits it was his idea to use Rich's ex-wife, Denise, a major financial contributor to the Democratic party, as a means of influencing Clinton.

On September 10th, The Washington Times rW1S a story by Rowan Scarborough entitled, "U.S. Troops Would Enforce Peace Under Army Study." This article focuses on a 68-page paper by the Army School of Advanced Military Studies (SAMS), which looks at a variety of issues including different military agencies and their modus operandi. Of the Massad, the Israeli intelligence service, the SAMS officers state,

"Wildcard. Ruthless and cunning. Has capability to target **U.S.** forces and make it look like a Palestinian! Arab act."

On September 11th, the attack on the World Trade Center and the Pentagon is orchestrated by Israel with the complicity of British and America, under the orders of the Rothschilds, which they in turn blame on so called Muslim terrorists. This is Stage One of getting the Western World to go to war with the Arab World, on behalf of the Zionists. Another textbook Mossad false flag operation, remember their motto,

"By Way Of Deception, Thou Shalt Do War"

They also will use the attacks to gain control of the few nations in the world who don't allow Rothschild central banks, and so, less than one month after these attacks, United States forces attack Afghanistan, one of only seven nations in the world that does not have a Rothschild controlled central bank. These nations are all predominantly populated by Muslims who, unlike the majority of White Christians (see Nehemiah 5:7), obey their scripture and refuse to partake in the lending or borrowing of money, "usury," something which has riled the imposters for hundreds of years.

The Zionists are also most unhappy with Muslims throughout the world. This is because the plan to destroy the Muslim faith that worked so well or the Zions with regard to the Christian faith has largely failed.

The Zionists worked hard to get Muslims to migrate into many Western nations, the plan being that they would forget their religious beliefs and become nothing but consumers of Zionist owned products, services and governments, like the majority of the white Christian world.

The Synagogue of Satan, ISBN 978-1-930004-45-0
To contact the author.
Andrew Carrington Hitchcock invites you to contact, him at: *andrewcarringtonhitchcock@hotmail.com* or go to his website: *www.thesynagogueofsatan.com*

still further, one would assume, given the fact that an intelligence summary for Condoleezza Rice from CIA Director George Tenet on June 28 said: "It is highly likely that a significant al-Qaeda attack is in the near future, within several weeks."[17] It was in such a context that the rather specific warnings came.

In late July, for example, the Taliban's Foreign Minister informed US officials that Osama bin Laden was planning a "huge attack" inside America that was imminent and would kill thousands.[18] That the information indicated that the attack was to involve commercial airlines is suggested by the fact that on July 26, CBS News reported that Attorney General Ashcroft had decided to quit using this mode of travel because of a threat assessment—although "neither the FBI nor the Justice Department...would identify what the threat was, when it was detected or who made it."[19] In May of 2002, it was claimed that the threat assessment had nothing to do with al-Qaeda, but Ashcroft, according to the Associated Press, walked out of his office rather than answer questions about it. The San Francisco Chronicle complained: "The FBI obviously knew something was in the wind.... The FBI did advise Ashcroft to stay off commercial aircraft. The rest of us just had to take our chances." CBS's Dan Rather later asked, with regard to this warning: "Why wasn't it shared with the public at large?"[20]

August and September brought more warnings. A Moroccan agent who had penetrated al-Qaeda was evidently brought to the United States to discuss his report that bin Laden, being disappointed that the 1993 bombing had not toppled the WTC, planned "large scale operations in New York in the summer or fall of 2001."[21] Former CIA agent Robert Baer reportedly told the CIA's Counter-Terrorism Center that he had learned from a military associate of a Persian Gulf prince that a "spectacular terrorist operation" was about to take place.[22] Some warnings, furthermore, were reportedly given by several foreign intelligence agencies. For example, Russian President Putin later stated that in August, "I ordered my intelligence to warn President Bush in the strongest terms that 25 terrorists were getting ready to attack the US, including important government buildings like the Pentagon." The head of Russian intelligence also said: "We had clearly warned them" on several occasions, but they "did not pay the necessary attention."[23] Warnings were also reportedly given by Jordan, Egypt, and Israel,[24] with the latter

country warning, a few days before 9/11, that perhaps 200 terrorists linked to Osama bin Laden were "preparing a big operation."[25]

One of the official warnings during this period became widely known—a memo provided by Great Britain, which was included in the intelligence briefing for President Bush on August 6. This warning said that al-Qaeda had planned an attack in the United States involving multiple airplane hijackings. The White House kept this warning secret, with the president repeatedly claiming after 9/11 that he had received no warning of any kind. But on May 15, 2002, CBS Evening News revealed the existence of this memo from British intelligence. Condoleezza Rice tried to dismiss its significance by saying that it was "fuzzy and thin," consisting of only a page and a half. Newspaper accounts, however, said that it was 11 pages long.[26] Press Secretary Ari Fleischer said in no uncertain terms: "The president did not—not—receive information about the use of airplanes as missiles by suicide bombers."[27] A few days later, however, the Guardian reported that "the [August 6] memo left little doubt that the hijacked airliners were intended for use as missiles and that intended targets were to be inside the US."[28] Doubt about the administration's truthfulness is raised by the fact that it has refused to release the memo while claiming that there is nothing specific in it. As Michael Moore has asked: "If there is nothing specific, then why can't they release it?"[29]

In any case, if that information is still considered too general to have made the events of 9/11 preventable, even more specific information was provided by the stock market. Intelligence agencies monitor the stock market, critics point out, to watch for clues of impending catastrophes. And the days just before September 11 saw an extremely high volume of "put options" purchased for the stock of Morgan Stanley Dean Witter, which occupied 22 stories of the World Trade Center, and for United and American Airlines, the two airlines used in the attacks.[30] For these two airlines, and only these two, "the level of these trades was up by 1,200 percent in the three days prior to the World Trade Center attacks."[31] To buy a put option is to bet that the price of shares is going to go down, and in this case the bet was highly profitable. As the San Francisco Chronicle explained: "When the stock prices...dropped...in response to the terrorist attacks, the options multiplied a hundredfold in value, making millions of dollars in profit." If a single group of speculators

The MASTER PLAN
to ENSLAVE California,
the Americas and the World!
by Pat Revere

California is the <u>fifth largest economy in the world</u>. The MASTER PLANNERS want California very badly, because, once California is populated with local and immigrant volunteer SLAVES, (voluntary servitude), they can be put to work in the THREE BASIC INDUSTRIES which the MASTER PLANNERS now control.

The THREE BASIC INDUSTRIES are the KEY to the MASTER PLANNERS success. Every civilization, today and throughout history, has HAD TO HAVE these THREE BASIC INDUSTRIES in order to function, they are:

1. Agriculture, (now MASTER PLAN controlled)

2. Mining, (now MASTER PLAN controlled)

3. Fishing, (now MASTER PLAN controlled)

Taking control of these THREE BASIC INDUSTRIES over the past 97+ years, (a land grab), was fairly easy for the MASTER PLANERS. Getting the "persons"/SLAVES to "work" (voluntarily contract) into these THREE BASIC INDUSTRIES has been more difficult, however, the SLAVE trade is moving right along.

It is called, "illegal" immigration. It works well, as long as the MASTER PLANERS can keep the good People, (sui juris inhabitants), in the dark – keep them confused and keep them fighting among themselves. Then, the good People give up and move away, leaving a void to be filled by "illegal" immigrants and the already-on-welfare local SLAVES. The "illegal" immigrants are ALLOWED to continue to swarm over the borders, into their new SLAVE-STATE of California, and other states.

When these "illegal" immigrants arrive, their first order of business is FOOD STAMPS and WELFARE contracts. These contracts also allow them to, "register to VOTE." They SIGN up, (signature = volunteer into contract = SLAVERY). They believe there is NO pay-back – WRONG, they are signing a contract for the life-long SLAVERY of themselves, their children, their grandchildren and their grandchildren's children. The GOLDEN GOOSE, in actuality, is the SLAVERY goose!

Now, armed with the "GREEN CARD", which says they are a RESIDENT ALIEN, this card (contract) also says they are a U.S. citizen (small c citizen). This small c U.S. citizen looks official, and they think they have finally arrived in the good old US of A, WRONG AGAIN!

To keep this writing in understandable order, the following list of "legal", (WORD GAME), words is necessary. Most good Americans are not aware of this LAW BOOK WORD GAME which fraudulently tricks you into VOLUNTARY SERVITUDE or SLAVERY, they are:

Person   =   A corporate "thing" or chattel, i.e. a SLAVE (any contract you sign could be simply changed from person to People whenever the word person appears).

Resident   =   You reside in Washington, D.C., Puerto Rico, Guam, Mariana Islands, American Samoa, or other "U.S." territories, (if you do NOT live in any of these places, BUT, if you sign a contract saying you are a RESIDENT or ADDRESS or RESIDE, you have said that you DO in fact RESIDE there, then THEY have "GOT YOU", tricked you into a voluntary SLAVE contract). You may wish to strike the words RESIDENT or ADDRESS or RESIDE, changing them to – LOCATION.

Sui Juris   =   Free Man, (two words, this also includes the gals).

<u>U.S. citizen</u> = the Corporate U.S. "DEMOCRACY" government who <u>contracts</u> with volunteering SLAVES. YES, there are TWO governments operating here! To avoid the SLAVE government, you and I must declare ourselves as a Citizen, (<u>C</u>apital <u>C</u> Citizen), of one of the several states, (spell out the name of your state, DO NOT abbreviate), of the united States of America who recognizes the Constitution of the united States of America, (a REPUBLIC, NOT a DEMOCRACY), and its irrevocable/un-repealable "TEN" BILL OF RIGHTS. <u>U.S. citizens</u> do NOT have the Constitutional Rights they thought they had!

Unrevealed, NOT fully disclosed, <u>CONTRACTS</u> you may have <u>signed</u> in the past, are FRAUD. You may sue for damages at ANY date in the future. In the meantime, a simple letter rescinding your <u>signature</u> from that <u>CONTRACT</u> may do the job, and you can sue later. Remember, the most IMPORTANT thing you own ON THE FACE OF THIS EARTH is your <u>signature</u>!

The following is a partial list of several FRAUDULENT, unrevealed <u>CONTRACTS</u>, you may:

Cancel all unrevealed contracts with corporate government agencies, including –
but NOT limited to the following:

1. Cancel Voter Registration Contract,
   (you become a qualified elector).
2. Cancel Birth Certificate Contract,
   (family record is all that is needed).
3. Cancel Marriage License Contract,
   (Marriage Certificate is all you need).
4. Cancel <u>Driver</u> License Contract,
   (return to your birthright to <u>travel</u>).
5. Cancel Social Security Contract.
   (it has always been a voluntary failure).

So, what can a true blue American do about undoing the most sophisticated MASTER PLAN ever to be attempted for the ENSLAVEMENT of California, the Americas and the World?

To start, you have to KNOW and understand who is behind it and how this carefully planned, long range MASTER PLAN is being conducted.

Once you have a grasp on this, you can begin to cancel the unrevealed, FRAUDULENT CONTRACTS by rescinding your signature from these CONTRACTS. Usually, a properly worded letter, sent Registered Mail, can work well, (NO return receipt is suggested, it may be another contract).

Next, you can become familiar with the MASTER PLANNERS organizational control methods. When you do, you will see clearly how they control the government agencies as well as both PROFIT and NON-profit CORPORATIONS. Then, you will see how to correct and LAWFULLY PUNISH the MASTER PLANNERS for their HIGH CRIMES.

NOTE: (You may wish to contact the LOCATION at the end of this writing for the MASTER PLANNER control methods and THEIR PUNISHMENT).

It is a MUST to understand the MASTER PLANNERS' clever "end runs" around our Constitution which have taken place over many generations, such as the NOW DOCUMENTED EVIDENCE that the original 1819 13th Amendment* to our Constitution was REPLACED following the Civil War in 1865. This REPLACEMENT 13th Amendment confusingly mentions INVOLUNTARY SERVITUDE/SLAVERY, and is followed shortly thereafter by THEIR, (forcefully, improperly ratified), 14th Amendment, which mentions a "U.S. citizen" for the first time, (a corporate, voluntary SLAVE),

i.e., You VOLUNTEER INTO SLAVERY when you SIGN ANY CONTRACT WHICH STATES you are a U.S. citizen! You can also Lawfully volunteer OUT of this CONTRACT by rescinding your signature!!

* "Titles' of Nobility" Amendment

By returning to the original 1819, 13th Amendment to the Constitution of the united States of America, known as the TITLES OF NOBILITY Amendment, ALL elected officials, with "BAR ASSOCIATION" membership and ALL other TITLES OF NOBILITY, will IMMEDIATELY loose their citizenship/Citizenship and IMMEDIATELY be removed from office!

BAR ASSOCIATION "Attorneys" have been told throughout their law school experience, "you must pass the BAR examination before you can practice law" – NOT TRUE! This same PRIVATE "LICENSING" FRAUD takes place with medical doctors and others who have been continuously and intentionally LIED TO as part of the MASTER PLAN for a carefully PLANNED, totally controlled SLAVERY of all People.

The BAR ASSOCIATION, (both federal and state), and the AMERICAN MEDICAL ASSOCIATION memberships are PRIVATE "LICENSE" CONTRACTS and can be Lawfully avoided!

To reinforce – "Knowledge is power", which MUST be used for GOOD, Sheriff Richard Mack, of Safford, Arizona, said it best when he stated, "If you don't know your RIGHTS you can't use them, and if you know your RIGHTS and don't use them – YOU LOOSE THEM!"

REMEMBER, the MOST IMPORTANT thing you own ON THE FACE OF THIS EARTH is your signature…

* Now, get busy and help to Bring America Back *

MASTER PLANNERS, your days are numbered!!!

Write for a list of simplified and very understandable action materials:

America Publications

UK Becomes Police State

England perfecting surveillance of it own citizens

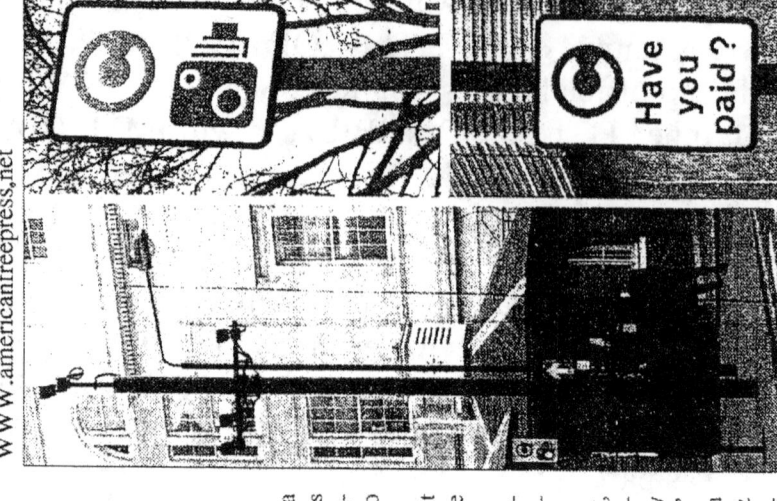

WWW.americanfreepress.net

By George Kadar

L ONDON—It is difficult to know how the average British citizen thinks and feels about critical issues in England because the voice of the average British citizen is long suppressed. British media outlets and policemen incessantly cite the growing threat of terrorism in all public forums.

England has emerged as the most perfected, technologically advanced police state in the world. Every major city in the country is fully covered with video cameras watching every main road. Even in the smaller cities, a "terrorist" can trigger an impressive display of flashing lights in the intersections by driving over the speed limit. And every British citizen can expect paper tickets with heavy fines to follow in the mail.

Every good citizen has to pay a $300 "TV tax" per year, and the few who do not own a television set at home are under constant mail attacks by the tax collector to explain why they do not pay this tax. The agency is perfecting an electronic device that is able to determine from the street if illegal television watching is taking place inside a home.

The gas and electricity meters in the homes will shut off the service when one runs out of prepaid credit. You then have to run to the nearest store with a small electronic gadget to prepay the gas or electricity so you can finish your hot shower.

Even the streets of small towns are turned into a jungle of paid parking spaces. The government needs every penny of revenue it can get to fund the installation of more cameras, monitoring devices and to pay for more snooping technology.

Policemen lurk on the streets with computers that recognize cars with unpaid road taxes; the cars are towed and released after heavy fines are paid.

The latest item is the "Dreambox" from Senstar-Stellar "providing information on the status of security devices, threats and suspicious activity."

But the real hot thing comes from Fleet Consult, Ltd. A small electronic gadget is attached to company cars that records every trip that's made. "We now have 100% accurate recording of all our vehicles' business miles. We know now that the information we have to give to Her Majesty's Revenue & Customs is absolutely correct." Not a small achievement if we consider that gasoline sells for around $7 per gallon.

And, unfortunately, the English seem daily ever willing to sacrifice more and more of their privacy in order to make England "safe for democracy."   ★

HAVE YOU PAID? Top left, Orwellian *1984* big-brother-style cameras monitor pedestrian and vehicle movements in London with sophisticated computers that read vehicle license plates in an attempt to ensure that not one citizen evades the fines. Other cities in England employ similar surveillance systems. Tickets are mailed (as they are here in the United States for light-running and speeding) to those whom the camera catches committing infractions or those who are not up to date on the payment of traffic fines, taxes etc. Here in the United

---

George Kadar is a European correspondent for *American Free Press*. A Hungarian national, he now resides in London. Mr. Kadar can be reached via email at kennewickanand@onviet.hu or by sending a letter c/o *American Free Press*.

POPULATION REDUCTION
(U.S. State Department <u>Global 2000 Report</u> of July 24, 1980).

THE WORLD DOES <u>NOT</u> HAVE AN OVERPOPULATION PROBLEM.

1. The advanced technology the world has been given will support many times the existing 5 billion population of this earth; however, this technology is being intentionally suppressed and withheld by the power mongers.

2. The estimated 5 billion people on this earth today could all be placed within the borders of the state of Texas with 549.3 square feet of private space for each man, woman and child!

On July 24, 1980, the U.S. State Department unveiled the *Global 2000 Report to the President*. It had been in preparation by the White House Council on Environmental Quality and the State Department, employing scores of government personnel and hundreds of outside consultants since the early days of the Carter administration—an administration dominated by elite members of David Rockefeller's Trilateral Commission. The report was a long-winded proposal that "population control"—a euphemism for killing people—be made the cornerstone of the policies of all U.S. Presidents from that time forward.

Pervading the report and several companion documents were lurid predictions: crises in water resources, severe energy shortages, shortfalls in strategically vital raw materials—all blamed on "population growth." The report argued that without countervailing action, by the year 2000 there will be 2 to 4 billion people too many. Therefore, the report said, it is required that government implicitly direct all policies domestic and foreign <u>toward the elimination of 2 to 4 billion people by the year 2000.</u>

The rationale for proposing a crime of such great magnitude is the simple—and totally wrong—Malthusian ideology that claims population growth inherently exhausts "natural resources" and that there are, therefore, "limits to growth," as the Club of Rome has insisted.

In other words, the *Global 2000 Report* is simply a statement of a policy intent for genocide, not a scientific forecast at all. It reveals in a unique way the depopulation aims of those also behind the ozone-depletion hoax.

By the time *Global 2000* was issued, whole sections of the U.S. government existed solely to implement its recommendation: depopulation. The role of Richard Elliott Benedick, who negotiated the Montreal Protocol for the United States, must be emphasized again. Benedick has spent most of his government career as head of the State Department Population Office, promoting policies to reduce the size of the world's population.

Next Comes Genocide

In 1989, Egyptian President Hosni Mubarak estimated that 500 million people in the Third World had starved to death in the decade of the 1980s; current estimates by the United Nations Children's Emergency Fund (UNICEF) are that <u>40,000 children under the age of five starve to death every day.</u> Most of these deaths can be attributed directly or indirectly to debt service and "technological apartheid," policies that prevent modern technologies—such as water treatment plants, nuclear energy, refrigeration, mechanized agriculture, <u>pesticides, and fertilizers</u>—from being used in Third World countries. These policies were considered colonialist in past decades; today, they are promoted by environmental groups in industrialized nations, under the guise of saving the Earth from pollution.

Many environmentalists have no idea of the consequences of their belief system for the people of the Third World, but it is clear that those at the top of the environmentalist movement are witting in their advocacy of policies that ultimately kill people. We know this is the case because many of the environmentalist policy-makers say so publicly. It is not simply that the ban on CFCs will kill people and that the top environmentalists know that it will kill people. The fact is that the top ozone depletion propagandists at the World Wildlife Fund, the Club of Rome, the Population Crisis Committee/Draper Fund, and other elite bodies *want* it to kill people. Depopulation is one of the reasons they devised the ozone hoax in the first place. By scaring the general population with stories of imminent catastrophe, these policy-makers intend to justify adoption of stringent measures that will curtail economic growth and population. The ozone hole is just one of several such scare stories.

UNITED NATIONS TREATY agenda !

The report neglects to point out that if science and technology were not to be forced into stagnation, the globe's population would have much brighter prospects.

DDT is NOT cancer causing. (malaria was almost irradicated when the DDT" scare went out !)

LET'S FIX IT!

79

POPULATION REDUCTION – the methods
(U.S. State Department <u>Global 2000 Report</u> of July 24, 1980).
by Pat Revere

First, the Global 2000 reporters set out to make you believe we have a over-population problem – when, in fact we DO NOT!

Next, the Global 2000 reporter/supporters, (the NEW WORLD ORDER "SELECT FEW" in charge, along with their DUPED appeasers), set out "quietly" to promote the elimination of 2 to 4 BILLION lives on this earth. This, because their BEAST computer kept telling them they could not maintain total control, "unless population is kept at level 2.5 BILLION worldwide." Note: The President of Egypt caught on to this scam in 1989 – and he was quickly murdered!!

The following is a partial list of their secretly orchestrated, and NOW EXPOSED, People Genocide, or mass-planned MURDER:

1. TECHNOLOGY – intentional withholding of technology from third world countries, i.e., DDT (Not cancer causing) and freon, (NOT damaging to the ozone layer above the earth, etc.). 500 MILLION third world people, (of ALL ages), died unnecessarily during the 1980s.

2. HOMOSEXUALITY / PORNOGRAPHY – promotion of homosexuality and pornography as alternate sexual lifestyles, i.e., sex education (how to) classes and government (pro-homo) regulations. This results in NO children, NO family and then DEATH of a family line – in ONE generation.

3. CHEMICAL AND BIOLOGICAL WEAPONS – resulting in quick or long term death. Many believe these weapons have been in use for many years – including possible, slow acting, additives to Polio and other vaccines as well as Operation Desert Storm <u>syndrome</u>.

4. ANTIBIOTICS / PRESCRIPTION DRUGS – the pharmaceutical company executives will not use most of their own company products, (except for occasional "one time" showbiz), could they be slow death?

5. PROCESSED FOODS – processing of food cooks out oxygen and vital life support nutrients from ALL foods, causing illness and slow death. Fresh foods could be in abundance without government "crop restrictions" and regulatory controls.

6. "ILLEGAL" DRUGS – government drug promotion and highly suspect government drug dealing is on a worldwide scale. Drug education, (how to) school classes, have PROVEN they PROMOTE drug use (and early death) among children and others.

7. REFINED SUGAR – refined sugar (poison) consumption is SLOW DEATH. Natural sweeteners including honey are still around.

8. ASPARTAME – the Federal Drug Administration, "FDA", approved this slow death poison in 1974. ASPARTAME poison is in ALL artificial sweeteners. Those of the FDA who approved ASPARTAME, now hold, or have held high paying jobs with the artificial sweetener companies after leaving the FDA. You can be sure they knowingly never use this poison – WHY did they do that?

9. FLUORIDE – is slow death, a government promoted poison added to drinking water as well as toothpaste, vitamin pills and rat poison.

10. CHLORINE – a slow death poison added to municipal water supplies. Most doctors will tell you NOT to consume chlorine because it is poisonous. Some worldwide water supplies are now treated with the harmless, very disinfectant OZONE treatment, good idea!!!

11. ABORTION OF UNBORN BABIES – since 1963, this abomination known as MURDER has deprived America of a major part of its next several generations.

12. SUICIDES – faithless people are committing suicides in epidemic numbers, "by GLOBAL 2000 design." Stresses, caused by CONTROLLED NEWS MEDIA – (negative, SHOCK news), INTERNAL REVENUE SERVICE – (collection agency threats of financial destruction) and GOVERNMENT LAW ENFORCEMENT AGENCIES – (regulatory, unlawful attacks on the populous), are causing great numbers of suicides among the faithless, worldwide.

THERE IS
   NO
   WORLDWIDE
   OVERPOPULATION

STRAIGHT TALK ON SPP

By Congressman Ron Paul

Globalists and one-world promoters never seem to tire of coming up with ways to undermine the sovereignty of the United States. The most recent attempt comes in the form the misnamed "Security and Prosperity Partnership of North America" (SPP). In reality, this new "partnership" will likely make us far less secure and certainly less prosperous.

According to the U.S. government web site dedicated to the project, the SPP is neither a treaty nor a formal agreement. Rather, it is a "dialogue" launched by the heads of state of Canada, Mexico and the U.S. at a summit in Waco, TX, in March, 2005.

What is a "dialogue"? We don't know. What we do know, however, is that congressional oversight of what might be one of the most significant developments in recent history is non-existent. Congress has had no role at all in a "dialogue" that many see as a plan for a North American Union.

According to the SPP web site, this "dialogue" will create new supra-national organizations to "coordinate" border security, health policy, economic and trade policy, and energy policy between the governments of Mexico, Canada and the U.S. As such, it is but an extension of NAFTA and CAFTA-like agreements that have far less to do with the free movements of goods and services than they do with government coordination and management of international trade.

Critics of Nafta and Cafta warned at the time that the agreements were actually a move toward more government control over international trade and an eventual merging of North America into a border-free area. Proponents of these agreements dismissed this as preposterous and conspiratorial. Now we see that the criticisms appear to be justified.

Let's examine just a couple of the many troubling statements on the U.S. governments SPP web site: "We affirm our commitment to strengthen regulatory cooperation. . . and to have our central regulatory agencies complete a trilateral regulatory cooperation framework by 2007."

Though the Bush administration insists that the SPP does not undermine U.S. sovereignty, how else can one take statements like this? How can establishing "trilateral regulatory cooperation" not undermine our national sovereignty? The web site also states SPP's goal to "improve the health of our indigenous people through targeted bilateral and/or trilateral activities, including in health promotion, health education, disease prevention and research." Who can read this and not see massive foreign aid transferred from the U.S. taxpayer to foreign governments and well-connected private companies?

Also alarming are SPP pledges to "work toward the identification and adoption of the best practices relating to the registration of medical products." That sounds like the much-criticized *CODEX ALIMENTARIUS,* which seeks to radically limit America's health freedom.

Even more troubling are reports that under this new "partnership", a massive highway is being built, stretching from Mexico to Canada, through the state of Texas. This is likely to cost U.S. taxpayers untold billions of dollars, will require eminent domain takings on an almost unimaginable scale, and will make the U.S. more vulnerable to those who seek to enter our country to do us harm.

This all adds up to not only more and bigger government, but to the establishment of an unelected mega-government. As the SPP web site itself admits, "the SPP represents a broad and ambitious agenda". I hope my colleagues in Congress and the American citizens will join me in opposing any "broad and ambitious" effort to undermine the security and sovereignty of the United States.

Ron Paul (R) represents the 14th District of Texas.
To show your support for Ron call his office at: 888-322-1414, or visit his web site at: www.ronpaul.org.

North Bridge NEWS

November 1995   Published by *The Liberty Tree*   Anthony Wayne, Editor   Volume 1, Issue 14

The Unknown $9.1 Trillion Company

The Depository Trust Company (DTC) is the best kept secret in America. Headquartered at 55 Water Street in New York City, this "financial institution" is perhaps the most powerful in the world, yet the public doesn't have a clue as to who they are or what they do. How can a "bank" hold assets of over 9 trillion dollars and be unknown?

In dealing with the trust department of a major New Jersey bank, one of our staff wanted to transfer his trust assets, comprising of stocks and bonds, to a new trust he had set up in another state. The bank said it would take at least 6 weeks to do so as none of his assets were currently held in his own name or in the name of his trust account! In a panic, he brought this before our entire staff and asked if we could investigate. We did, and the can of worms we've opened should frighten every American.

After encountering numerous "no comments" and a myriad of "that's not my department" excuses, we eventually spoke with Mr. Jim McNeff, Director of Training at the DTC. He says he's been employed there for 19 years and was very proud of his employer. By law, he should have disclosed to us that his employer(?) was recording our telephone conversation (our electronic equipment picked up on this immediately).

He informed us that **"DTC is the largest limited trust company in the world with assets of 9.1 trillion"**. Can you imagine? An unknown banking company could pay off the national debt and then some! Jeff went on to say **"DTC is a brokerage clearing firm and transfer center. We're a private bank for securities. We handle the** book entry transactions for all banks and brokers. Every bank and brokerage firm must secure their membership with us in case they become insolvent, so your assets are secure with DTC".** Yes, you read that correctly. DTC is a private entity that processes every stock and bond (paper securities) for all U.S. banks and brokerage houses. The big question is 'just who gave this company such a broad range of financial power and clout'?

The reason the public doesn't know about DTC is that they're a private depository bank for institutional and brokerage firms only. They process all of their book entry settlement transactions. Jeff told us **"There's no need for the public to know about us... it's required by the Federal Reserve that DTC handle all transactions"**. The Federal Reserve Corporation is a private company, not an agency of our federal government. They mandated that DTC process every securities transaction in the US. It's no wonder that the DTC is owned by the same stockholders as the Federal Reserve Corporation. In other words, the Depository Trust Company is really a front for the Federal Reserve Corporation. Now, let's see how this effects the average working American.

You go to a broker or bank and instruct them you want to purchase 100 shares of IBM stock, for example. They set up an account for you and act as your agent with power of attorney to conduct business on your behalf, upon your buy or sell instructions. The broker will place your stock or bond purchase into their safekeeping(?) under a "street name". (According to DTC, no bank or broker can place the stock into their firm's own name due to Federal Trade Commission and Security and Exchange Commission regulations).

The broker or bank must then send the transaction to the DTC for "ledger posting" or "book entry settlement" under mandate by the Federal Reserve Corporation. Remember, since your bank or broker can't use their name on the certificate, they use a fictitious entity name or "street name". This artificial entity is always related to the broker or bank. Then, the "street name" stock or bond certificate is automatically transferred to, or credited to, the Depository Trust Company. Since DTC is a bank, they can't hold the certificate in their name either, so DTC transfers the certificate to their own holding company or "nominee name". We're not quite sure of the spelling, but the DTC's holding company is either "CD and Company" or "CeDe and Company".

The banks and brokers are merely "custodians". By federal law, they cannot hold any assets in your name, the customer. The assets must to be held, eventually, in the name of DTC's holding company. That's how DTC has 9.1 trillion dollars of assets in trust... or is it really in "trust" if the private Federal Reserve Corporation is technically holding it in their "unknown" entity's name? Obviously, if stock and bond certificates you've purchased aren't in your name, then the "holder" (the Federal Reserve Corporation) could theoretically refuse to surrender them back to you under a "national emergency" according to the 1917 Trading with the Enemy Act. Is

(Continued on page 2)

Norton v. Shelby County

18 US 425 p. 442

An unconstitutional act is not law; it confers no rights; it imposes no duties; affords no protection; it creates no office; it is in legal contemplation, as inoperative as though it had never been passed.

(Continued from page 1)
this the collateral being held by the private Federal Reserve Corporation to pay off the national debt owed to them by our federal government?

According to Mr. McNeff, the DTC was a former member of the New York Stock Exchange (NYSE), and **"Our sister company is the National Securities Clearing Corporation"**. Simply put, the Depository Trust Company absolutely controls every paper asset transaction in America, and they physically hold the majority of stock and bond certificates in their name. If you have stock or bonds in your name buried in your back yard or under your mattress, we suggest you keep them there.

Now we're about to reveal to you the most shocking discovery we've ever come across during our research into this matter. Most of us remember a few years back the alleged "computerized" selling of stocks that resulted in "Black Monday". The stock exchanges had dramatic record losses, and a record volume of shares was traded on that infamous Monday in October. We all asked ourselves how computers could have done this by themselves without someone knowing about it. After all, someone has to program a computer to tell it what to do and when to do it.

During our telephone conversation, Mr. McNeff was trying to assure our researcher that they have never lost a certificate or made a mistake in a book ledger transaction. In attempting to give us an example of how trustworthy they are, he said **"DTC's first controlled test was 4 or 5 years ago. Do you remember Black Monday? There were 535 million transactions on Monday, and 400 million transactions on Tuesday"**. He was very proud to inform us that **"DTC cleared every transaction without a single glitch!"**. Read these quotes again. He stated that "Black Monday" was a controlled test! "Black Monday" was a deliberately manipulated disaster for many Americans at the whim of a "controlled test" by the DTC and their Federal Reserve Corporation owners.

What was the purpose of this test? Common sense tells us that you test something before you intend to use it.

It's quite obvious that the stock markets are going to crash and burn at some future date and for some unknown reason since the controlled test was so successful. The Great Depression is about to be repeated, and it will be as deliberate and manipulated as the first one that began with the stock market crash of 1929.

On June 7, 1995, the federal government issued a new regulation requiring stock and bond certificate transfers to be cleared in three days instead of the previous five day time period. This means that brokers and banks must get your stock or bond transaction into the name of DTC within 3 working days. That's hard to do considering banks claim that it takes 3 or more days to clear a check that you've submitted to pay for a stock purchase. But, there's a reason for this new regulation and it coincides with the introduction of the new fiat "dollars".

On February 22, 1996, **"the DTC will flip the switch"** according to Mr. McNeff. What switch, we asked? This is the day that "clearing house" funds will no longer be accepted for stock or bond transactions. Instead, only "Fed Funds" will be accepted. Fed Funds, or a "Fed Wire", are electronic ledger transfers between Federal Reserve Corporation member banks. No checks or drafts will be involved or allowed from that day on. This is called a "cashless transaction". We call it the reality of the "mark of the beast". This is the manifestation of our new god, the New World Order.

Consider this. All pension funds and other institutional "managed funds" are comprised of paper asset investments such as stocks and bonds. These certificates are technically in the name of DTC's private holding company. DTC is technically owned by the private Federal Reserve Corporation. Congress is moving right now to pass legislation allowing certain pension funds to be used by the government as alleged loans. All the Federal Reserve Corporation has to do is hand it over! But what happens to the people counting on those pension fund investments to feed themselves? Too bad... you're out of luck because for the "good of the nation", you must share your wealth. Since the Federal Reserve Corporation already holds

our stocks and bonds in their fictitious name, then perhaps they'll cash them in for the federal government's failure to repay the loans that have become way overdue.

In 1933, all gold was taken from the hands of private citizens. Under the War Powers Act, a national emergency was declared due to the deliberately calculated stock market crash that preceded the Great Depression. Where did this gold end up? Into the hands of the Federal Reserve Corporation. The majority is stored in the impervious rock beneath New York City. Is it any surprise that DTC holds our stock and bond certificates in the same place?

Technically, our entire nation is still under the War Powers Act and in a continual state of national emergency. The President can enforce any new emergency at any time under Executive Order or Presidential Directive. On or about February 22, 1996, expect a new national emergency to be declared. They'll blame it on the infamous drug dealers who are allegedly destroying our currency. Old dollars will be called in and exchanged for new ones. If you don't do it within a given time period, you may be sent to prison if you're caught. This is what happened to those Americans holding gold after 1933.

This national emergency will most likely call for the confiscation of all gold bullion again. Who will end up with it? The Federal Reserve Corporation, just like before. Then, perhaps they'll peg the new dollar to gold prices, as many experts have already reported. What will stocks and bonds purchased with old dollars be worth then? Pennies on the dollar, so to speak. Who ends up being the _only_ winner? The Federal Reserve Corporation stockholders.

People will be at the mercy of the government for daily food and for jobs. Without a Fed Fund ATM type card you won't be able to transact business, get your food ration, or pay for the electric bill. Checks will be phased out totally during 1996. The switch is being turned on in February. This is not speculation! This is the truth of reality. It's already been tested, and their new system works.

The day has come when you must decide to accept or reject the beast.

The Horrors of our Judicial Treason

There exists a very public international conspiracy to destroy the United States of America from within. Ruled by ungodly lawyers and lawyer/judges of the numerous national and international Bar Associations, their judicial system has created unconstitutional aristocratic courts ruled by "esquires" wearing black robes of Nobility. This has created Ruling Class courts of nobility in direct violation of our Constitution.

"No Title of Nobility shall be granted by the United States: And no Person holding any Office of Profit or Trust under them, shall, without the Consent of Congress, accept of any present, Emolument, Office, or Title, of any kind whatever, from any King, Prince, or foreign State." -Article I, Section 9 of The Constitution for the United States of America.

The existence of these unconstitutional Ruling Class Courts is not new to our nation. *We the People* have accepted them and allowed them to flourish just as blindly as sheep merrily going to slaughter... and the slaughter of Rights, Liberty and Freedom is exactly what has come about. The lawyers have taken over not just our Judicial Branch, but the Legislative as well. For example, try to name just one member of Congress who has neither attended law school nor is a Bar lawyer. Good luck on your search because a non-lawyer Congressman is a rare species. As for the Executive Branch, lawyers abound in the office of the Presidency.

If all three Branches of our government are controlled by lawyers, who is representing *We the People*? The truth is, these are the terrorists who are in control of our government and have eliminated our Constitution. The threat is real and the takeover is complete. Right now, this minute, we are ruled not by a republican form of government but by a Ruling Class of self-proclaimed Nobility.

"The United States shall guarantee to every State in this Union a Republican Form of Government..." -Article IV, Section 4 of The Constitution for the United States of America.

Neither the word LAWYER nor the word ATTORNEY appear anywhere within our Constitution. This was no accident on the part of our Founding Fathers. They had been cruelly subjected to ungodly Courts of Nobility from a Ruling Class of Aristocrats, and they deliberately framed our Constitution to prohibit such a thing from ever surfacing within this land again by creating three distinct and separate Branches of Government. Today, ALL lawyers are automatically members of the Judicial Branch due to their unconstitutional Title of Nobility.

"No State shall... grant any Title of Nobility." -Article I, Section 10 of The Constitution for the United States of America.

We the People must be elected or hired to be in any government branch, but <u>all</u> "Bar" lawyers are automatically "Officers of the Court" of the Judicial Branch of government. Then, whenever a lawyer is hired or elected to the Executive or Legislative Branches, he holds an office in two Branches of our government at the same time. This is blatantly UNconstitutional and in violation of the separation of powers, checks and balances, and conflict of interest laws. Perhaps now *We the People* can see how we've allowed these lawyers of treason to rule our nation.

In our Constitutional Republic, <u>nothing</u> is to be above *We the People* other than God Himself. Then why have we allowed a Ruling Class of Nobility Title to have power over us? *We the People* are guilty of allowing our Constitutional Republic to fade away into non-existence. WE are the reason the ungodly lawyers rule our governments. WE allowed it. WE are responsible. WE are the only Constitutional power that can change it. <u>How could we have forgotten that ALL people in a Constitutional Republic are sovereign</u>?

If you enter into an ungodly and unconstitutional private Bar lawyer and lawyer/judge court (such as county, circuit, and state courts), you can be held in "Contempt of Court" for absolutely <u>any</u>

reason what-so-ever. The robed lawyer/judge does not have to follow any rules or guidelines to throw you into prison for alleged contempt against his wishes. In such a case, there is **no arrest** made, **no due process of law** (in violation of the 14th Amendment), **no bail, no Habeas Corpus**, there is **no prosecutor, no jury, no trial** (much like a lynching), and you have **no Rights**. The lawyer/judge is your **accuser**, your **prosecutor**, and he <u>alone</u> **convicts** and **sentences** you <u>without a trial</u>. Such an act of imprisonment is called a **BILL OF ATTAINDER** (see Article I, Sections 9 & 10) and is <u>absolutely</u> <u>unconstitutional</u>, yet it happens every single day hundreds of times.

Then the lawyer/judge orders a law enforcement officer to imprison you, even though that law officer has sworn under oath to support the U. S. Constitution. This is no less than a lawyer lynching, and every law officer should refuse to obey such an illegal order. No law officer is obligated to obey any illegal law or order, such as a Contempt of Court Order.

It's very odd how most forms of organized crime in America, such as the Mafia, never thrived at great lengths until the bar lawyers took over our courts and our governments. The "courts" have protected their activities, if the price was right. Crime syndicates are organized internationally in the same way as the Bar Associations. Just what is the purpose behind the **World Assembly of Judges**, the **World Peace through Law Center**, the **International Trial Lawyers Association**, and the **International Judicial Association**?

Their purpose is the New World Order. All nations must now comply with international standards these organizations have set up. The entire world is under no less than lawyer mandated justice administered through the United Nations. The Constitution for the United States is no longer in effect. You and I have no Constitutional Rights. Instead, we have privileges granted by those who dare to call themselves "esquire".

America's 62 year old Constitutional Dictatorship

National Emergency: A state of national crisis; a situation demanding immediate and extraordinary national or federal action- Black's Law Dictionary.

"I think of all the damnable heresies that have ever been suggested in connection with the Constitution, the doctrine of emergency is the worst. It means that when Congress declares an emergency, there is no Constitution... for when this bill becomes a law, ...there is no longer any workable Constitution to keep the Congress within the limits of its Constitutional powers." -Spoken by Congressman Beck in 1933 prior to the passage of the Farm Bill.

Once an emergency is declared, there is no Constitution. Senate Report 93-549 (written by Congress in 1973) states in the very first sentence *"Since March the 9th, 1933, the United States has been in a state of declared national emergency. Under the powers delegated by these statutes, the President may: seize property; organize and control the means of production; seize commodities; assign military forces abroad; institute martial law; seize and control all transportation and communication; regulate the operation of private enterprise; restrict travel; and... control the lives of all American citizens"*. This situation has continued absolutely uninterrupted since March 9, 1933. We have been in a state of declared national emergency for nearly 63 years without knowing it.

According to current laws, as found in 12 USC, Section 95(b), everything the President or the Secretary of the Treasury has done since March 4, 1933 is automatically approved: *"The actions, regulations, rules, licenses, orders and proclamations heretofore or hereafter taken, promulgated, made, or issued by the President of the United States or the Secretary of the Treasury since March the 4th, 1933, pursuant to the authority conferred by Subsection (b) of Section 5 of the Act of October 6th, 1917, as amended [12 USCS Sec. 95a], are hereby approved and confirmed. (Mar. 9, 1933, c. 1, Title 1, Sec. 1, 48 Stat. 1]"*.

On March 4, 1933, Franklin D. Roosevelt was inaugurated as President. On March 9, 1933, Congress approved, in a special session, his Proclamation 2038 that became known as the Act of March 9, 1933: *"Be it enacted by the Senate and the House of Representatives of the United States of America in Congress assembled, That the Congress hereby declares that a serious national emergency exists and that it is imperatively necessary speedily to put into effect remedies of uniform national application"*. This is an example of the Rule of Necessity, a rule of law where necessity knows no law. This rule was invoked to remove the authority of the Constitution. Chapter 1, Title 1, Section 48, Statute 1 of this Act of March 9, 1933 is the exact same wording as Title 12, USC 95(b) quoted earlier, proving that we are still under the "Rule of Necessity" in a declared state of national emergency.

12 USC 95(b) refers to the authority granted in the Act of October 6, 1917 (a/k/a The Trading with the Enemy Act or War Powers Act) which was *"An Act to define, regulate, and punish trading with the enemy, and for other purposes"*. This Act originally excluded citizens of the United States, but in the Act of March 9, 1933, Section 2 amended this to include *"any person within the United States or anyplace subject to the jurisdiction thereof"*. It was here that every American citizen literally became an enemy to the United States government under declaration.

According to the current Memorandum of American Cases and Recent English Cases on The Law of Trading With the Enemy, we have no personal Rights at law in any court, and all Rights of an enemy (all American citizens are all declared enemies) to sue in the courts are suspended, whereby the public good must prevail over private gain. This also provides for the taking over of enemy private property. Now we know why we no longer receive allodial freehold title to our land... as enemies, our property is no longer ours to have.

The only way we can do business or any type of legal trade is to obtain permission from our government by means of a license.

So who initiated all of these emergency powers? On March 3, 1933, the Federal Reserve Bank of New York adopted a resolution stating that the withdrawal of currency and gold from the banks had created a national emergency, and *"the Federal Reserve Board is hereby requested to urge the President of the United States to declare a bank holiday, Saturday March 4, and Monday, March 6"*. Roosevelt was told to close down the banking system. He did so with Proclamation 2039 under the excuse of alleged unwarranted hoarding of gold by Americans. Then with Proclamation 2040, he declared on March 9, 1933 the existence of a national bank emergency whereas *"all Proclamations heretofore or hereafter issued by the President pursuant to the authority conferred by section 5(b) of the Act of October 6, 1917, as amended, are approved and confirmed"*.

Once an emergency is declared, there is no common law and the Constitution is abolished. We are no longer under law. Law has been abolished. We are under a system of War Powers. Our stocks, bonds, houses, and land can be seized as Americans are considered enemies of the state. What we have is not ours under the War Powers given to the President.

Whenever any President proclaims that the national emergency has ended, all War Powers shall cease to be in effect. Congress can do nothing without the President's signature because Congress granted him these emergency powers. For over 60 years, no President has been willing to give up this extraordinary power and terminate the original proclamation. Americans are an enemy subject to tribunal district courts under Admiralty wartime jurisdiction; a Constitutional Dictatorship.

If the Constitution doesn't say they can do it – then it is 100% illegal.

The average age of the world's greatest civilizations has been 200 years. These nations have progressed through this sequence: From bondage to spiritual faith; from spiritual faith to great courage; from courage to liberty; from liberty to abundance; from abundance to selfishness; from selfishness to complacency; from complacency to apathy; from apathy to dependency; from dependency back into bondage.

This is America today!

How much government do free people need?

From: "Chuck Baldwin Live"
chuck@chuckbaldwinlive.com
via Duane Smith
duane.smith@seligmannet.com

People (and courts) today define liberty as the exercise of uncontrolled passions. However, the unrestricted exercise of debauchery serves only to assail -- not assist -- freedom.

This is a parent who Rapes his or her child!

As John Adams said, "We have no government armed with power capable of contending with human passions unbridled by morality and religion. Avarice, ambition, revenge would break the strongest cords of our Constitution as a whale goes through a net. Our Constitution was made only for a moral and religious people. It is wholly inadequate to the government of any other."

Without inward morality, constitutional government is totally non-existent.

The rule of constitutional law over the affairs of men is absolutely dependent upon the rule of divine law within men's hearts.

Assaults on liberty

The McAlvany Intelligence Advisor
Box 84904 / Phoenix, Arizona 85071

In this century, three presidents in particular -- Woodrow Wilson, Franklin D. Roosevelt, and Lyndon B. Johnson -- have successfully launched fundamental assaults on America's heritage of Constitutional liberty. None of their successors altered the course on which these presidents directed us.

Neither Harding, Coolidge nor Hoover undid the damage done during the Wilson presidency. Eisenhower consolidated and extended the systems put in place under FDR's New Deal and carried forward the institutional policies of the Truman presidency.

When Richard Nixon became president, instead of challenging the neo-Marxist revolutionary agenda of LBJ's Great Society, he consolidated it and extended it, while providing increased funding for its activities.

An armed people is safer

Resurrection, The Newsletter

"To trust arms in the hands of the people at large has, in Europe, been believed . . . to be an experiment fraught only with danger. Here by a long trial it has been proved to be perfectly harmless . . . If the government be equitable; if it be reasonable in its exactions; if proper attention be paid to the education of children in knowledge and religion, few men will be disposed to use arms, unless for their amusement, and for the defense of themselves and their country."

• Timothy Dwight, Travels in New England and New York (London, 1823)

Has Arizona become a fascist 'police state'?

East Valley Tribune, May 1, 2001

"Arizonans had better stand up quickly and let their elected officials know how they feel about recent court rulings of they are in for a sad, sad surprise. Citizens are now handcuffed in shackles and handcuffs for zoning violations and now they can be arrested for minor violations and handcuffed. Is this really what we are paying taxes for?"

Thank you "RVP" and Staff – RVPaper, Box 867, Eagar, Arizona 85925

SOLUTIONS – Fax these notices and offers far and wide.

ENTER THE STRAWMAN

You have been, and are right now, the unknowing victim of an ingenious, though ancient diabolical conspiracy of untold ramifications. Americans are under undeclared martial law rule, and have been since Abraham Lincoln declared martial law in 1861 and took over the government and congress as Commander-in-Chief of the Armed Forces of the United States. Unknown to most of us, all property ownership is in the hands of the state, the United States ·Corporation (the federal zone, Inc.) - Washington DC.

You do not own the property that you think you own - not your home, your vehicle, or even your children! The state can take away your children and your other property (chattel) if you do not behave as the state sees fit, regardless of the Constitution, the Bill of Rights and the Common Law. All property in America belongs to the state, just as the plank in the Communist Manifesto regarding property ownership declares. The state has "legal title" to all property while we have only an "equitable interest" in what we think we own, and that only on our "good behavior". As long as we give tribute (excessive tax money) to the conquering state, they will leave us alone to enjoy life and "liberty".

As a slave on the king's plantation, we work for him only, via the Company Store - *the non-federal* Federal Reserve. The slave is subject to his master, and the created is subject to its creator. The state has created our "Strawman", assigned him a Social Security Nr., and presumes that we have unknowingly agreed (contracted) to be the surety (co-signer) for him. "Our" S.S.# is not our 1.0. but the 1.0. of our Straw-man. The state deals only with our Strawman. If our Strawman is fined, we have to pay our Strawman's fine. All our bills come to our Strawman written in its all-capital lettered "war trade-name" which sounds exactly like our real name when spoken. "JOHN Q. DOE" does not mean the same in law as "John Quincy Doe".

All commerce is conducted between the state and our Strawman. Our Strawman works not for us but for the state. He has no "standing-in-law" because he is a slave and his master is the state. We are his surety and the spokesman for what he does, with or without our consent.

Redeeming ourselves means we can contract to do whatever we want to do. We can even contract to redeem our invisibly contracted Strawman from government control so that he will work for us and no longer for the state. Like an item pawned to a pawn shop, out Strawman is waiting there for us to be redeemed. When we recapture our Strawman we regain commercial control of our life. We are now prince of the king and no longer his slave. The struggles, confusion, grievances, and financial exploitations are no more. The courts can no longer control us when we inform them who we are - *no Strawman,* but non-corporate, natural human beings - and no longer under the state's control.

The process of *Redemption-in-Law* or *Acceptance for Value* is a lawful restoration of our inherent status. But we have to make our new status publicly known. We give public notice of the redemption of our status by transferring our Strawman's birth certificate registration from the public corporate domain to the private <u>in</u>corporate domain. In other words, from the martial-rule <u>democracy</u> under which we now live to the common-law <u>republic</u> of the private side of life - via a UCC Financing Statement according to the Uniform Commercial Code.

You have just been introduced to a little known life-changing course of action that can liberate you from government duplicity. Democracy can be changed back to the republic for which our "red, white and blue flag of peace" stands - not their "gold-fringed flag-of-war." For additional information do a web search for *"Redemption In Law."*

SCOOPIFIED
P.O. Box 277
Bellingham, W A 98227

The National Educator

P. O. Box 333, 1051-E South Lemon, Fullerton, CA 92632
VOLUME 22, NO. 2 — ONE DOLLAR PER COPY — JULY, 1990

" (AND) TO THE REPUBLIC FOR WHICH IT STANDS"

A democracy or a republic?

CORPORATE↘
NATIONAL

CONSTITUTIONAL↘
↗FEDERAL

*

THE SOLDIERS TRAINING MANUAL *

issued by the War Department, November 30, 1928, set forth the exact and truthful definitions of a democracy, and of a republic.

TM2000-25: 118-120
DEMOCRACY:

A government of the masses.
Authority derived through mass meeting or any other form of direct expression.
Results in mobocracy.
Attitude toward property is communistic-negating property rights.
Attitude toward law is that the will of the majority shall regulate, whether it be based upon deliberation or governed by passion, prejudice, and impulse, without restraint or regard to consequences.
Results in demagogism, license, agitation, discontent, anarchy.

Bad!

TM 2000-25: 120-121
REPUBLIC:

Authority is derived through the election by the people of public officials best fitted to represent them.
Attitude toward property is respect for laws and individual rights, and a sensible economic procedure.
Attitude toward law is the administration of justice in accord with fixed principles and established evidence, with a strict regard to consequences.
A greater number of citizens and extent of territory may be brought within its compass.
Avoids the dangerous extreme of either tyranny or mobocracy. Results in statesmanship, liberty, reason, justice, contentment, and progress.

Good!

* This training manual for soldiers no longer teaches our fighting men

what a Republic is –

Republic is what we all want – Democracy is what we have !
(GOOD)   (BAD)

(The "plan" began calling America a "Democracy" in the 1920s)
(What became of –"and to the Republic for which it stands" ?)

LET'S FIX IT!

Epilogue

The Synagogue of Satan can be expected to continue its centuries-old global assault on Christian civilization. The Moslem world is also under intense attack. The plan of the (Zionist imposters) is to divide and conquer, to have Christians and Moslems at each others throats and thereby to destroy both.

The ultimate goal is a fasco-socialist New World Order, a (Zionist imposters) Utopia, and a global system of concentration labor camps alongside wealthy (Zionist) enclaves.

Whether the Synagogue of Satan achieves this diabolical goal is up to you. Yes, God's will shall eventually be done. His plan shall prevail. But the question is, what does God require of you and me, now, today? Will we, with God's help, successfully fight and overcome evil, or instead, will we passively submit to the monstrous crimes of the greatest array of criminals the world has ever known-the talmudist overseers who comprise the Synagogue of Satan?

The Synagogue of Satan; ISBN 978-1-930004-45-0

To contact the author:
Andrew Carrington Hitchcock invites you to contact him at: *andrewcarringtonhitchcock@hotmail.com,* or go to his website: *www.thesynagogueofsatan.com*

The Power of One

Author Unknown

One song can spark a moment,
One flower can wake the dream.
One tree can start a forest,
One bird can herald spring.

One smile begins a friendship,
One handclasp lifts a soul.
One star can guide a ship at sea,
One word can frame the goal.

One vote can change a nation,
One sunbeam lights a room.
One candle wipes out darkness,
One laugh will conquer gloom.

One step must start each journey,
One word must start each prayer.
Our hope will raise our spirits,
One touch can show you care.

One voice can speak with wisdom,
One heart can know what's true,
One life can make the difference,
You see, it's up to you!

"God plus one = a majority" ☺

* * * **Warning** * * *

We are ALL guilty of allowing
GRADUALISM **/** SOCIALISM
to slowly take over America
by forming a "corporate" United States.

This material will possibly

shock you into a state
of partial or total DENIAL,
REJECTION and ANGER
you WILL recover!

When you do, GET BUSY,
BREAK the "CODE OF SILENCE"
and help bring the REAL
America back - at God's Speed

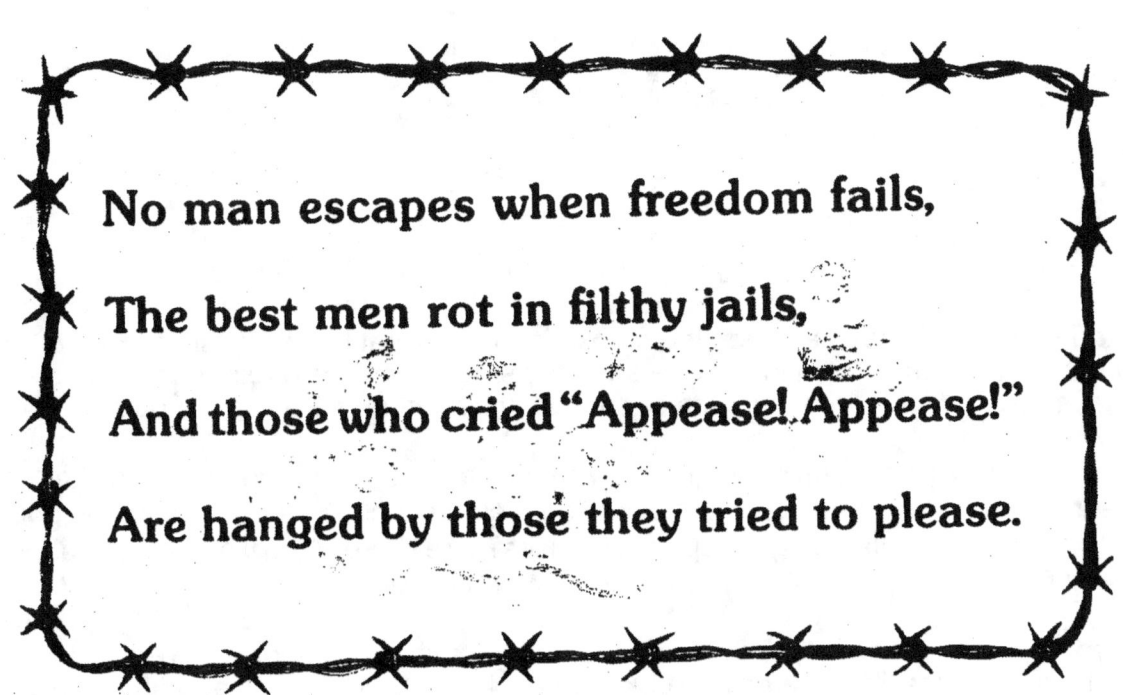

No man escapes when freedom fails,

The best men rot in filthy jails,

And those who cried "Appease! Appease!"

Are hanged by those they tried to please.

one or two

CAN

make the difference !

LET'S FIX IT !!

?   Blue Sky   ?

I am seeing less and less of the real deep lovely clear blue sky anymore.

I asked someone if they had seen the smoke in the sky that looks like some kind of sky-writing and that someone said, "I have seen the smoke and it is airplanes putting out some kind of smoky chemical that spreads out and stays in the air for a very long time."

I think I know what a "vapor trail" is. It's when a fast jet plane, way up high, has a little white trail coming off its wings which disappears almost right away. What then is going on with these smoky trails being let out in our skies? Are there dangerous chemicals in this smoke? Does the smoke (or chemicals) come down in rain?

I found some people the other day who seemed to have some good answers to my questions. Answers like, "we have pictures of airplanes lacing our skies with white smoke-like chemicals. They also said, "we believe these chemical trails are dangerous to people and plants as well as cutting out sunlight." Then they added, "There are people allover North America, in the cities and in the country, who have been collecting rain water which is discolored from the chemical trails." They said, "we believe these chemicals are killing many trees and plants and are a major cause of people having more and more lung congestion."

When I asked these people if they had asked the government or the military what was going on with smoky chemical trails in our sky's, they said they had inquired and that they had received answers such as, "what chemical trails?'

I have seen lots of these smoky chemical trails in the past several months over Arizona skies and I really miss the crystal blue sky I used to see often.

My big question is who are the pilots of the airplanes spreading smoky chemical trails in our skies? Who are the people loading these airplanes with these chemicals? Are their jobs so important that they will obey any order or request from their supervisor or boss even though they know that what they are doing is probably against the law?

I am a very upset American who would like my blue sky back! I would like to see these smoky chemical trails stopped IMMEDIATLEY!

More information?
www.arizonaskywatch.com or call (602)404-0847
www.californiaskywatch.com or call (707)485-7520
www.hyperstealth.comlhaarp/index.htm

THE FOLLOWING PUBLICATIONS ARE AVAILABLE
(Prices include shipping & handling)
Money Order To: America Publications
3370 N. Hayden Rd., Ste. 148
Scottsdale, Arizona 85251

1. THE FAREWELL by President George Washington $12.00
   (his timeless farewell address), 19 Sept. 1796 A.D.
   (New-table of contents by subject & color prints of GW and Martha).

2. 101 WORDS $10.00
   From the Unanimous Declaration (of Independents)
   Words you MUST know in order to understand it. !
   Declaration and 1828 definitions included.

3. EVIDENCE OF THE MISSING 1819 ORIGINAL 13th AMENDEMENT $12.00
   Two RARE publications have been re-discovered. Confirming
   Its Lawful proper ratification, re: "TITLES OF NOBILITY."

4. CITIZENS RULE BOOK (pocket size, color cover) $5.00
   Includes- Declaration of Independence, Constitution, Bill of Rights,
   Amendments, Jury Rights and much more.

5. SILENT WEAPONS FOR QUIET WARS $14.00
   (World War III started in 1954)
   The enemy manual for the "Quite War" they have almost won.
   Found by accident at an auction in 1986.

6. EMERGENCY POWERS, ACTS OF WAR $10.00
   Two Americans formally charge the living Presidents with TREASON!
   Complete with boiler plate Affidavit and all documents.

7. THE SWISS REPORT $12.00
   By Gen. George Patton, U.S.A. and Gen. Lewis Walt, U.S.M.C.
   The Swiss Civilian Militia keeping the peace for over 400 years.

8. ALL ABOUT THE UNITED NATIONS SUBVERSION FROM CHARTER TO FLAG $15.00
   Complete with CHARTER, TREATY and repair documents.

9. SHOWDOWN AT NEW RIVER $12.00
   BATF " invasion" of New River, Arizona.
   A UNITED community FIGHTS BACK and WINS!

10. UN / IMF ENEMIES OF THE PEOPLE $12.00
    The PRE planned attempt of TOTAL worldwide control/ slavery,
    WHO is behind it and HOW to STOP and CORRECT it.

11. GOOD NEWS about DRINKING WATER $10.00
    The most reliable and economical pure drinking
    Water info. With solutions for better health.

12. KILLERBEE- HONEYBEES ARE HERE, DON'T PANIC $10.00
    Bees play a very necessary part in the food supply.
    Learn how to avoid these bees while not destroying them.

13. TO LIVE AGAIN $16.00
    Courageous first persons stories of overcoming
    drug, sex and alcohol addictions, with solutions.